D1389825

SHANE

SHANE
MY STORY

Shane Williams
and Delme Parfitt

MAINSTREAM
PUBLISHING

EDINBURGH AND LONDON

First published in Great Britain in 2008 by
MAINSTREAM PUBLISHING COMPANY
(EDINBURGH) LTD
7 Albany Street
Edinburgh EH1 3UG

ISBN 9781845963675

A catalogue record for this book is available
from the British Library

Typeset in Billboard and Caslon

Printed in the UK by CPI William Clowes
Beccles NR34 7TL

ACKNOWLEDGEMENTS

MANY THANKS to Huw and Ben Evans for providing the photographs for this book.

CONTENTS

1

BATTLING THE BOKS

I ALWAYS think that the sign of a truly great sports person is one who never wallows in his or her own success. I am reminded of something Sir Alex Ferguson said after Manchester United won the Champions League final against Chelsea in Moscow: he said that the sweet taste of victory was like a drug to him but that its effects wore off quickly, and he soon needed another fix.

Then there are people such as Tiger Woods and Roger Federer, who crave more and more titles, no matter how many they win. And, of course, there is our own Joe Calzaghe, who despite being a world champion for more than ten years has always adopted the mantra of training like a challenger.

It's an attitude that marks all of them out from the rest, and I am just grateful that it is an outlook that has now seeped into the Welsh rugby team. We enjoyed the success of the 2008 Six Nations, and we celebrated it fully, but when it came to touring South Africa in the summer afterwards, we all very much wanted to draw a line under what had gone before and to challenge ourselves at an even greater level.

Warren Gatland underlined that kind of thinking to us when we first met up ahead of the tour to take on the world champions on their own soil. He talked about drawing a line in the sand and not dwelling on the Six Nations just gone, saying that it was meaningless in the context of what lay ahead. He told us that we had to continue to strive and not to think that there was not plenty of room for improvement. Warren made it clear that for all the pats on the back for the Grand Slam success, there were a number of things in that tournament that we hadn't done well. He said he wasn't interested in us being a good side; he wanted us to be a great one. And he finished by stressing that in his opinion we were more than capable of going to South Africa and winning.

I think his words hit home, especially to those of us who had experience of the peaks and troughs of the past. For example, in the aftermath of the 2005 Grand Slam, the Wales team had failed to take the next step and ended up back in the doldrums the following year, when we had hoped to build on the achievement and to make it the springboard for a new era of success.

We were not under any illusions before we left for our training base in Cape Town. The bottom line was that the standard in South Africa would be a different kettle of fish altogether from taking on our usual northern-hemisphere foes – and we had to be ready for it or face embarrassment.

Ultimately, it was a disappointing trip because we didn't come back with what we wanted: a first-ever win on Springbok soil. But – and I know this next phrase has become a bit of a cliché in rugby circles – there were positives for us to take from it.

Undoubtedly the biggest downer of the whole tour was the performance in the first Test, which we lost 43–17 in Bloemfontein. Why were we so poor? Well, I just can't explain it. I know that we prepared thoroughly and trained well in the days leading up to it. But the performance was hideous.

I've looked back at that match since, and the number of handling errors we committed was staggering – they were at a level that is always going to ensure you lose a Test match against even moderate opposition, never mind the world champions. I could barely recognise us at times. I was shocked. Warren didn't mince his words to the media after that match. He said we were embarrassing and that we had been humiliated. He got it spot on. There was no point trying to offer up any flannel.

It hadn't been easy for us, in that we had been together only a week beforehand. On top of that, we had Lee Byrne, Gavin Henson, Dwayne Peel, Mike Phillips and Martyn Williams all out injured and therefore had quite a few new faces to integrate into the group. But if we're honest with ourselves, we had no real excuses.

The tour began in a special way. We stopped off at Clarence House in central London for a reception with Prince Charles in recognition of our Grand Slam, and it was a pretty memorable occasion.

We got lost on the way, at one stage getting into a terrible muddle near Piccadilly that forced us to do a U-turn in our huge bus. That in turn prompted a couple of police outriders to come and take us to our destination. It was an incident that typified a Welsh rugby tour, and we ended up being half an hour late.

There were a huge number of security personnel and police when we arrived, and just before we got off the bus our team manager, Alan Phillips, gave us final instructions in how we were to address the prince, which was to call him 'Your Royal Highness' in the first instance and then 'Sir' thereafter. As I said, there were a huge number of security and police about, and Charles was never once without a couple of minders right next to him, even though it was hardly as if any of us were going to wrestle him to the floor.

Although Charles is a member of the Royal Family, I can reveal that he does know his rugby. You could tell that he hadn't just been told what to say by someone else beforehand. His interest and knowledge were obviously genuine. I thought that was great, because while I was understandably nervous before meeting him, especially in that kind of environment, the way Charles chatted put me at ease. To be honest, he just came over as a normal bloke. It was the second time I'd met him, as I'd crossed his path at the Millennium Stadium a few years earlier, but this was my first opportunity to have a conversation with him.

I have found Prince William to be the same as his father. He has attended quite a few of our games and has popped into the dressing-room afterwards to chat to us. I suppose it's a bit surreal to have a member of the Royal Family in there, what with us sitting in a steamy room, some half-naked, with bits of mud and strapping strewn about the place. But you're just so tired at those times that you barely give it a second thought. And, again, what has struck me is just how normal William is. He just speaks to you like you are one of the lads, which is great. On occasion, he has been teased by some of the boys, who have asked him if he fancies coming out for a beer with us that night, but he takes it all in his stride. It must be difficult for him, because he is a normal guy who can never live a normal life.

To be at Clarence House that day before setting off to South Africa, though, was a real eye-opener. I expected it to be posh, but the sheer magnificence of the decor really hit home, with paintings, ornaments and grandfather clocks everywhere, and the food they put on was so nice that half the time I barely knew what I was eating! It was nice to experience something like that.

Charles asked me how I coped playing rugby at international level when I was so small. I thought that was quite a nice way to get the conversation started and an understandable question, and he finished by telling me to take care in South Africa 'because they're big lads!'

He went around a lot of people, though. He asked the fitness coaches about training, telling them he had a bad back and had to be careful what he did. Then we gathered together for some photographs before leaving for Heathrow.

By that point, there was a real sense of being on a mission. Touring can be tough mentally as well as on the field, and being away from home for long periods is something I have had to get used to. I find it harder these days now that I have a wife and young daughter to leave behind. When I was young, I had nothing to miss. Because I lived alone, I had far less to come back to.

I hate missing out on my daughter Georgie growing up, even if I am only away for two and a half weeks, as I was for the trip to South Africa. Every time I come back, she has changed in some way, and it makes me think. Two weeks is long enough for me these days. The Lions trips that last seven or eight weeks are killers – but you don't complain too loudly, because those are the ones you want to be on. In my experience, the boys are all different – some like getting away from their wives; others miss home as soon as we touch down – but I guess we all have to accept that it is part and parcel of the job we have chosen to do.

We were straight into training when we reached South Africa, arriving there in the morning and then having a light session that afternoon at our training base in Cape Town. We decided to stay there until the day before the first Test in Bloemfontein, because the advice we had was that it was the best way to cope with the altitude we would encounter on the Highveld.

Cape Town is quite a dangerous place, but at least you can go out and about there in a way you cannot in other places in South Africa. When you go on tour, you are there to do a job, but you need time to yourself as well – time to switch off and appreciate the country you have visited. Doing that enables you to stay fresh for when it is time to get down to business.

One afternoon, a group of us went swimming with sharks, which was something I had always wanted to do, and it was an unforgettable experience. I love anything to do with nature and wildlife, and I'm forever glued to the Discovery Channel, watching all manner of programmes. I kept a pet snake when I used to live on my own – a boa constrictor to be precise. It turned out to be one of the craziest things I have ever done, and it didn't work out. It all started when a mate of mine said that he knew a guy who was looking to pass on the snake, as he and his wife had just had a baby – I guess babies and boa constrictors aren't exactly a match made in heaven. I agreed to give it a new home, but it turned out to be a nasty old thing. I kept it for about six months in a special tank in my lounge. I don't think it helped that my mates used to annoy it whenever they came round because it was so unusual.

At the start, I used to get it out of the tank and drape it around my shoulders, but that had to stop after a while because it seemed like it was getting more vicious by the day. It got to the point that every time I walked past the tank it would try to go for me through the glass. That was when I decided to get rid of it, giving it away to an enthusiast who kept a load of other reptiles. I had a chameleon once, too – I think it was probably out of loneliness.

The only animals I have at the moment are tropical fish, but my daughter Georgie wants a puppy, and although I have said no for now, conscious of what a commitment it is, she will probably get her way sooner or later. I suppose I'm a bit of a budding David Attenborough, really.

I've always been fascinated by sharks, and as soon as I knew we were off to South Africa I pencilled in a dive. There were about 18 of us who went out in the end, although some wouldn't risk it, Mark Jones and Matthew Rees, for example, telling us that we were nuts to go diving with great white sharks. What didn't help was that the morning we were due to go, Rhys Long, the squad's video-analysis man, turned up with his iPod and showed us video footage of a great white attacking a cage of divers and managing to get inside. Not surprisingly, that prompted a few doubts.

But there was no way I was pulling out. A lot of those who went didn't go in the water, and I didn't blame them, because when you go out and see these things in the flesh it is enough to put the wind up anybody. But I just found them fascinating rather than being scared of them. We didn't see any real monsters, but even the younger ones were big. And with the instructions of the guides not to stick so much as a little finger through the bars of the cage ringing in my ears, I couldn't help but be a little nervous, but it was something I am so glad I did – it was one of the most exciting experiences of my life.

We also took the chance to go out on safari on our day off before the second Test in Pretoria. I can recommend that to anyone. I got to see wildebeest, lions, ostriches, cheetahs, springboks, warthogs – just about everything, really. It truly made me appreciate the magic of South Africa.

I have been on tours when I have done next to nothing on our days off, just going to a shopping mall or the cinema, but this time, although my mind was firmly on the rugby before anything else, I knew what was available and was determined to come home with some life experiences as well. And it made the tour for me.

But days like that were just a small part of the package in South Africa. Anyone who has been there will know just how big rugby is in the country, with 60-feet high billboards of Bryan Habana everywhere, reminding you just who their superstars are. Rugby is an obsession, especially at a time when the national team are world champions, and the South African people, and their media in particular, are not exactly shy in telling you how good they think their team is. Grand Slam or no Grand Slam, we were not given a hope in hell by anyone from the moment we set foot on their soil. We were seen merely as a speed bump for the Boks – preparation for them ahead of the Tri Nations tournament. It wasn't a case of if the Boks would win, but by how much. And there was no escaping that attitude. It was everywhere we went. From day one, we were told that the Boks were stronger, that their fitness levels were better, and that their skills and game knowledge were superior.

I could also sense that opinion when I spoke to their press people, who saw us as cannon fodder, with all their coverage reflecting that. I think it annoyed everyone in our camp, but I know for a fact that it riled me. I was being called the Welsh Habana by some of their journalists and being asked what I thought it would be like to play against Bryan in a way that made me feel I was expected to feel privileged just to tread the same turf as their hero. It felt degrading, to be quite honest, and it spurred me on a bit more.

One of the first things Warren said after the opening press conference over there was that their media wasn't giving us a hope in hell, and I think that also stiffened his resolve to prove them wrong, to shove their words back down their throats.

Of course, all this just made the scale and manner of our first-Test defeat all the harder to bear. As I said before, it is difficult to account for such a dismal display. We trained very intensely, as we always do. We knew we had to front up physically, that it was going to be supremely tough in that area and that we would have to hold our own in the breakdown. We also knew that we had to keep the ball away from Bryan Habana, Tonderai Chavhanga and Conrad Jantjes, who are some of the most dangerous strike runners in the world.

But we couldn't back up any of those plans with actions when it mattered most. Instead of punching our weight in the arm-wrestle, we were bullied and conceded an appalling 18 turnovers. On top of that, our error count was shocking and so was our discipline, as we handed them 12 points on a plate through penalties in the early stages. We got the rough end of referee Dave Pearson's whistle, but we had only ourselves to blame.

Afterwards, I was absolutely furious. We had talked the talk all week, going on about the need to gain respect from the world champions and how we wanted to make the critics eat their words, but when push came to shove, we had failed miserably. In fact, all we had done was give extra weight to their claims about how ordinary we were.

Beforehand, I had felt really confident. I thought our forwards were ready to give as good as they got, and I was looking forward to being able to feed off quite a bit of ball. So much for that . . .

There was some straight talking in the dressing-room afterwards from Warren and Shaun Edwards, who told us the display had been embarrassing and that it simply wasn't good enough. They got no argument – we knew it was the truth. The disappointment was not so much the result but the fact that we didn't front up in any department, and I could sense the frustration amongst the players.

We were determined not to let it happen again in the second Test. There wasn't a hint of anyone letting their hair down that Saturday night; instead, we went out for something to eat, and then we all went straight to bed – not that I could sleep, though. I had the game running around in my head non-stop. I'd been on the wrong end of some bad defeats with Wales before that had got me really down, but the difference this time was the sheer anger I was feeling.

There was a bit of a fuss made about the try I had scored in the second half. I had found a bit of space down the left wing, got my legs going and stepped inside Bryan Habana on my way to the line. Of course, that was what people noticed – the fact that I had wrong-footed one of the superstars of the game – but if you want the truth, the score meant nothing to me because we had lost so pathetically and it hadn't influenced the game at all.

But if I was angry that night, it was nothing compared to how I was during the game. Looking back, I can barely recognise the way I behaved, such was my frustration. I was finding that I just wasn't getting the ball, and it was driving me round the bend. It seemed every time we got the ball in a good position and I thought that something might be on, we turned the ball over or made a mistake.

I ended up shouting my head off at the rest of the boys. At one stage, I yelled, 'Just give me the fucking ball and I'll score.' When I remembered it afterwards, I thought to myself, 'You idiot.' It was a cocky, arrogant thing to have said, and it is just not like me at all, but I suppose it was an indication of how desperate I was at the time. The other, darker, side of me definitely came out.

I even started abusing Habana. He came across to defend my side of the field later in the game, just as my anger was coming to the boil. I began shouting at him, 'Mismatch, mismatch!' I continued by shouting at our boys, 'Just give me the ball. I've got him easy. No problem!'

He didn't take kindly to it. 'Ah, fuck you, fuck you,' he yelled back at me.

I guess I just wanted the ball. I just wanted to put one over on Bryan Habana now that the game was effectively over. He wasn't very happy, but afterwards we had a laugh and a joke about it. We're mates at the end of the day, and I didn't even feel the need to apologise to him. In rugby, there is an understanding between players that passions sometimes rise on the field and lead to a few verbals. Everyone knows that there is nothing sinister in it. I just laugh about the way I acted when I think back now. It wasn't the Shane Williams I know.

I hope Bryan doesn't think any worse of me. If it's any consolation, I only behaved like that because of the respect I have for him. I'll admit it was an individual battle that I wanted to win, and with the game lost I thought I'd try and win the banter. But I lost it that day, big time. I was angry with myself, angry with the team, angry with the Springboks and angry with the scoreboard. It was one defeat that took quite a bit of getting over.

We didn't change that much going into the second Test, which might surprise a few people. We felt the problem wasn't so much how we approached the first game as how we executed everything we tried to do. That was what we needed to improve. On the odd occasion we had done things well, we felt we had put them under pressure. So the aim was just to go out at Loftus Versfeld and right a few wrongs, and that's basically what we did.

Training didn't change that much, but this time when it mattered we were so much more on the ball and switched on. In the end, we lost again, 37–21, but I don't think there's any doubt that the score flattered South Africa, and it was especially hard to take when they got a try right at the end.

We led 21–20 after about an hour, but we just weren't clinical enough to close the game out. What was telling for me was the substitutes they were able to bring on, players such as François Steyn, Andries Bekker, Percy Montgomery and Bismarck du Plessis, all top-class internationals who could fire them at a stage when our legs were tiring as a result of playing at altitude. We just didn't quite have the types of reserves they had in their squad. When you see people like that coming on for the last 20 minutes when you yourself are flagging, it is tough to take.

Much was made about the potential effects of playing at altitude. Well, it is obviously a factor. I felt it most at the start of the games as I was building up to getting my second wind. You just get this burning feeling in the lungs that you wouldn't get back in Wales. However, in my book, the altitude could never be used as an excuse for what happened. During the warm-up and the first ten or fifteen minutes, you can notice it, but then you get used to it, and it's not a problem. I actually felt really good after the games in terms of muscle soreness; the only pain I felt was because of a couple of bangs to the head.

There are few challenges quite like that of taking on South Africa in their own backyard, but by this stage of my career I kind of knew what to expect. They are big guys, and one time when Bakkies Botha hit me I saw stars. But I know all about what it is like to see stars by now.

It's clear we still have a way to go to reach the level of being able to beat teams such as South Africa, never mind doing it on their own soil. But the way we performed in the second Test leads me to believe that we do not have as far to go as some might originally have feared. I have played against the Boks on numerous occasions when, if I am honest, I have known before the game that we didn't really have a hope in hell of beating them, because they were clearly so superior to us. But before the second Test, I truly believed we could win, and I have never felt that strongly before. For me, it was the best we have ever competed with them.

We got to within two points of them in the autumn of 2004 at the Millennium Stadium, going down 38–36, but that day the score probably flattered us a little bit. It was only a late surge of points from us that narrowed the deficit, and they had bossed the whole game. But in Pretoria it had been different. We were in the lead on two separate occasions, including just after the hour mark, and it was far more of a ding-dong encounter. That is what we have to take out of it.

Of course, the tour didn't go too badly for me personally. As well as that score in the first Test, I got another try in the second game that ranks right up there as one of the best I have ever scored.

I do get asked every now and then to name my favourite all-time try that I have scored, but I find it impossible to single one out. All I can say is that there are a few that are grouped together in a higher echelon of touchdowns that I have been lucky enough to score. That one in Pretoria was definitely in that bracket.

It was all over before I could blink. Again, I was trying to get involved a bit more in the game, and when I pounced on a loose ball and found myself in space I never really gave it that much thought; in fact, very little tends to go through my head in the first split second of those situations. The first thing I had to do was gather the ball up off the floor and not knock it on, but once I managed that I was immediately aware of the fact that they had plenty of cover defence backtracking.

I got past John Smit, the hooker, first of all, and that was when I really pinned my ears back. I didn't think I would get there simply by running straight for the corner, so my plan was to step inside and see if there was anybody on my shoulder who

I could offload the ball to. But I realised almost immediately that none of our guys were near me, so I had an instant change of mind. As I went to step inside, I thought, 'Hold on a minute, the defender closest to me has turned his head away. If I can just change my angle a little bit, I might just get to the line.'

My instinct was correct. As soon as I stepped off my right foot and headed back towards the outside, I knew I was in. I didn't have much time to think – it was almost as if my legs were one step ahead of my mind. And what made it all the better was that the try meant something in the context of the game, unlike the one I'd scored in the first Test. It got us into the lead and wiped clean the points we had given them earlier on. Our tails were certainly up at that point, but it wasn't to be.

There was disappointment at losing at the end, as I felt that we were good enough to have won. I honestly thought a lot of the referee's decisions went unfairly against us that day, and I am not one to look to blame officials. It is doubly frustrating when that happens in a match like that because you are up against it enough as it is.

Overall, though, we were happy with the way we bounced back from the week before. We had gone out there looking to gain respect, and I think by the time we came home we had done that. But I will return to the theme I began with – there will be no resting on our laurels in this Wales team. Our culture will just not permit that. Neither the management nor the players will rest until we are in a position where we can beat teams like South Africa on a consistent basis. Only then can we ever be considered as realistic challengers for the World Cup, and that has to be the aim of a rugby nation like Wales. It has to be.

2

LITTLE TEARAWAY

I'VE ALWAYS lived in the Amman Valley, in and around Glanamman and Garnant. I am friends with the same people today as when I was young, and that's the real reason why I still live there now. My family consists of my mam, Christine, dad, Mark, younger brother, Dean, and younger sister by six years, Hayley, with Beth my youngest sister coming along much later when I was well into my teens.

My earliest memory of home life was living above a pub called The Cross Keys in Glanamman, which is still there now, and I still pop in from time to time. I suppose it was an unusual environment to grow up in – I certainly became very good at pool at a young age. I remember the old faces who used to drink there, such as the old boy Edgar, who would bring in some kind of toy for me every other week. There were a few others like him who have probably long since passed away, and they all took me under their wing. Some nights I'd even play cards with them.

My mother and father tell me to this day that I was a bit of a nutcase as a kid, a bit like my little daughter Georgie is now. They say I couldn't sit still for two minutes and often tipped pints over while darting around the pub, getting myself into mischief.

I was busy and into everything, sidestepping tables and chairs – maybe that's where I learned it all.

The Cross Keys was only a small place, and our living quarters were the same. It was one of these old-style smoky pubs, where the old boy sits in the corner with his pipe. There was a pool table, a dartboard and a smattering of frayed seats about the place, and that's the way the locals liked it. But when my brother Dean arrived, the upstairs became a bit too small for us.

I was happy there, very happy, and the unique smells of a pub have stayed in my nostrils for life. On the odd occasion I have found myself in a pub of a morning before opening time, the smells of stale tobacco and beer have turned my stomach. I used to see half-empty glasses with flat lager in them the morning after the night before as my mother cleaned up. It was a sight that I will never forget. Even now, if I have a pint with an inch or so left in it and it has been there slightly too long and gone flat, there is no way I can drink it.

We didn't stay at The Cross Keys that long. After a few years, we moved to a council estate in Glanamman and then on to nearby Penybont. I'm not entirely sure why we left the pub. Maybe it was because the lease ran out, or perhaps my mam and dad just grew tired of the place. But soon we were living out of a small two-bedroom house, with my mother trying to make ends meet doing whatever job she could find and my dad working as a long-distance lorry driver who spent weeks on end away in Europe.

I missed Dad terribly. Sometimes it felt like I wouldn't see him for months, and I had to get used to living with just Mam and Dean and Hayley. In fact, I saw very little of Dad while I was growing up, first because of his work, but then because my parents separated in 1984 when I was about seven. They were divorced two years later, in 1986.

Why do the years stick in my mind? Well, probably because it was something that affected me deeply. I was accustomed to seeing Dad hardly ever, but to me their separation meant I would all but never see him, which sent me into despair. I can't recall the actual moment Mam told me the news. I just know I was upset, even though Dad only moved to Brynamman, not far away, where he lived with my grandmother. Even so, whenever I went up to my grandparents, full of hope at the prospect of seeing him, he was hardly ever there because of his work. And these were the days when there were no mobile phones, which meant at the times I was desperate to reach him to talk to him about something, there was no way of doing it. That was hard to take.

I idolised my father. He was – and still is – quite a character in local parts. His nickname has always been Mark Header – 'Header' meaning nutcase, which tells you all you need to know about what a personality he is in the valley. Dad was a bit of a drinker and could be a bit of a brawler as well – the norm for guys in my valley. He worked hard and played hard and was seen as someone not to be messed with. I was proud of that. I was proud of his reputation, and I wanted his approval as well as his company.

It got me down when I would find out that he had been home for the weekend in Brynamman and had gone out drinking without seeing me. As I grew up, I would bump into his pals in the local shop or just out and about, and they would say, 'Hey, Shane, I was with your father at the weekend.'

'Were you? Oh great,' I would reply, pretending to be matter-of-fact about it, but deep down I struggled to contain the frustration that some bloke who meant nothing to me had spent time with my father and I hadn't seen him for a second. Worse, I'd not even known that he'd been home. The older I got, the more I became used to that scenario, though it got no less frustrating.

Dad was always pretty hard on me, though as he got older he mellowed. When I was young, he'd smack me for misbehaving, which was fairly regularly, given how busy I was as a child. I don't hold that against him in any way, though I don't condone smacking kids these days, either. It was different for me, though. It was just something I grew up with. I was treated firmly by my dad, and in later years when I had grown I sometimes gave Dad as good as I got – or at least tried to.

When I look back, I realise that he toughened me up. He was harder on me than my brother and sister simply because I was older and could take a slap better than them, but I believe his approach probably did me the world of good. What I will say is that growing up I always knew what was right and what was wrong, what I could get away with and what I couldn't.

There are things my parents did with me during my upbringing that I will try to use as a parent myself, but when it comes to discipline I won't be physical with my little girl because I personally don't see the need for it. You have to set down some rules with your children, but I find it so difficult with Georgie because if I give her a row, I can guarantee that five minutes later she'll be grinning at me with her big eyes, and I'll end up apologising to her.

Dad's approach probably hardened me for the knocks on the rugby field in later life, and I can remember taking to the physical side of rugby really well despite my small size. When I started playing as a young lad, it was Mam who was around and who would come and watch me play for the school team. My father never played rugby in his life, never did any sports and, as I say, was never really around. He did turn up on the touchline on the odd occasion, and at those times I really wanted to impress him.

As I was quite a hardy kid, I would play with older boys. For instance, I was in an Under-14 team when I was just 11, and things like that did impress my father. He loved the fact I could compete with lads who were far bigger than me. I could take a bang back then, and I would like to think I am the same now. I don't stay down easily on the pitch even if I am clattered by big forwards. I couldn't tell you the number of times I have been concussed or taken bangs to the head that have left me dazed for a good few minutes. But if I can, I will always get up and carry on with the game. I never want any opponent to think he has knocked the stuffing out of me, even if he has. I will always try to walk away and, if need be, coast for five minutes to get over it.

That is very much a philosophy of Shaun Edwards. He has openly said that he will only tolerate players staying down if they have a broken leg. He doesn't mean it literally, of course, but because you know that he would play on with broken bones – and actually did play one Challenge Cup final for Wigan with a broken cheek bone – then you think you should do it too.

I'm glad I had that attitude from an early age, but then again it was a time when you just had to make the best of everything, because there wasn't much to go around. At least in my world there wasn't.

In my younger days, it was Mam who would scrape together the money for a new pair of boots for me. Money was tight, and it wasn't like it is these days, with a direct debit going into her bank account every month from an absentee father. No, she received very little money from Dad. Yet Mam is a proud woman, and while it was difficult for her to work when we were young kids, she was a bit of a Del Boy-type character. She ducked and dived and somehow made ends meet, supporting us as best she could.

SHANE

We never really wanted for the necessities in life, but I never went on school trips, because we couldn't afford it, and if I was bought a school uniform, I would have to stick with the same outfit for the year. You probably think the trousers were halfway up my legs by the summer, but fortunately I never grew much, so I got away with it.

That was what we were used to. We never really had any money, although at the time I had no idea just how much my mother was struggling. Things like holidays abroad weren't even on our radar. If we ever did go away, it would be to a caravan in Pendine – my mother and us three kids. But summer holidays were never about going away for me. I was more than happy to spend 12 hours a day at a place known locally as 'The Tip', a small wooded area, where I could build dens and play 'fox and hounds'.

The Cwmamman United football ground was only across the way from where we lived, and we would play there for hours on end, ruining the surface and risking a rollicking from the committee. Then there was the local youth club. You could pay 20p and have the run of the place for the night, playing pool and table tennis, and there were discos on Friday nights and organised events such as canoeing or abseiling. We might not have been able to afford expensive things, but when I think back, everything we could possibly have wanted was there for us at the club and in the surrounding areas. We could never have an excuse for being bored.

Johnny Knockin' was another of my favourite pastimes – in other words, ringing the bell or knocking on the door of some poor soul and then legging it by the time they answered. We would gather together in a group and nominate one of us to go and do the knocking. Some of my friends actually relished the opportunity, but not me. I was always the first to run. In fact, half the time I was running before the door had even been knocked. The friends I did this with were the friends I went to primary and comprehensive school with, and I still hang around with them now. The valley is a bit like a twilight zone – it is as if time has stopped. So many of us have never moved away, but that's why I love it.

One thing I never went short of, thank goodness, was food, with my nan and gramps Mary and Emrys – my mother's parents – living nearby. I spent a lot of my time there, either staying for fairly long spells or going there every day after school. I also had a golden retriever for about ten years called Buckley, who was named after the bitter, which I remembered from my time living in the pub. I loved her so much. She used to come everywhere with me. But because I lived at my grandparents' for spells, that was where Buckley used to stay most of the time. It was great for Buckley there, as there was a lot of open land by the house, and she could have a bit of freedom.

When she died, I was devastated. I recall coming home from school when I was about 11 and finding out the news. There was a footpath and then a gate to another field before my gran's house, and Buckley always used to come to the footpath to meet me as I was on my way back. One day, she wasn't there, and straight away I was afraid something was wrong, as she was beginning to get on in years. All I can remember is sitting on the settee at my gran's after being told the news, sobbing my heart out. I don't think I stopped crying for days.

I can barely remember eating when I was a kid because I was always out and about on the go. I loved being outdoors, whatever the weather, and I used to go home just to have a drink of squash. And despite the warnings of my mother, I was almost always covered in mud.

Mary and Emrys only lived over the road from Glanamman Primary School, and when the bell went at the end of the day it was so often too tempting not to go to my grandparents, where I was invariably treated like royalty. Mary and Emrys are still with us. Thank God they are healthy, and I love them dearly. Their house was always a safe haven for me.

And sometimes I needed that safe haven. There are worse places I could have grown up, but there were parts of our estate that were rough, and I used to hang around with people who were three or four years older than me fairly often. There were numerous occasions when I had seven bells kicked out of me, and growing up with my brother probably didn't help on that front. Dean and I have always been close – always been like a double act. We still do a lot together, but when we were growing up, because I was three years his senior, I felt a bit like a parent to him at times. I felt very protective of him and got into God knows how many scrapes looking out for him.

Mind you, my size has shaped my character, too. Because I am small, I have had to punch above my weight all my life, with people seeing me as an easy target. I have had to learn not to take being pushed around, and for my brother it has been the same. Even now, nothing riles me more than people assuming that because I am small I will not be able to compete. It annoys me more than anything, and I would like to think that over my career I have proved that theory wrong.

Dean and I always shared a bedroom when we were younger, right up until I left home at the age of 18. The sizes of the houses we lived in gave us no choice. But while that forced us to get on, we fought like cat and dog at times. In fact, our punch-ups have become legendary throughout the valley.

Dean has one hell of a temper on him. Sometimes when he loses it, I fear he's going to turn into the Incredible Hulk. I have my breaking point, too, but I have a longer fuse. I am a bit cooler and calmer. Nowadays, we don't scrap anywhere near as much as we used to. We're more respectful of one another because of everything we have been through. But it hasn't always been like that.

One time, when I was about 14, we were having a barbecue in the back garden, and I was doing the cooking. Dean wanted to take over, but I wouldn't let him because it was too dangerous. Next thing I knew, he came at me from behind and punched me flat out on the back of my head. It was one of those punches that for a split second leaves you not knowing where you are and wondering, 'Did that really happen?'

When my head cleared, I flew into a rage with him, my fury made worse by the embarrassment that it had all taken place in front of my mate, Mark Hutchings. I picked Dean up, dragged him across the garden and threw him through the wooden panel of the back door to our house. Seconds later, I punched my fist through the glass to try and get at him again. Poor Mark was looking at the two of us in disbelief. Then, later, as we were standing outside, Dean started poking a barbecue skewer underneath the back door, hoping that he would make contact with my legs. Mark asked my mother if he could go home . . .

Down the years, Dean and I have had many a toe-to-toe. On many occasions, we've argued when we're out and agreed to go outside to sort it out with our fists. The last time was about three years ago. When it comes down to it, I am frightened to hurt him because the protective instincts of a big brother take over; however, the fact is that Dean is bigger than me these days and well capable of inflicting punishment on me.

In that last scrap, I had a cut lip, he had a bruised eye and both our noses were bleeding after we had slugged it out in front of our shocked friends. It stopped after we punched ourselves out, got tired and our mates managed to drag us off one another. Then we started arguing, he said something and I said, 'Yes, I agree with you.' Two minutes later, we shook hands and went back inside for a pint, where we ended up laughing about it – me with my split lip and him with his black eye. That is how it has always been. We have never argued or fought and then gone weeks without speaking to one another. It's crazy when you think about it.

You may not be surprised to know that I have a different relationship with my sister Hayley. She is just great with people. Everyone loves her, and we have barely ever had a cross word between us. She has always argued with Dean, but never me. Hayley works in the local doctors' surgery and part-time in the Amman United club as well. She's the type of girl who gets on with everybody. She has a three-year-old girl called Molly with her partner Carwyn, and she is just very happy with her life.

There's hardly anything Hayley won't do for me. She'll pick things up for me, or babysit Georgie, and it works both ways. She knows that I'll do all I can for her, too. We just have a great understanding. Hayley is the most down-to-earth girl you could meet, but she can have her crazy moments as well.

She's proud of everything I have done and likes to show her feelings. She's a more touchy-feely person than Dean or I will ever be. Dean will take the mick out of me if I do something good in rugby – the next time I see him, he'll pipe up with something like, 'Well, it's just a matter of time before it all comes crashing down!'

After the Ospreys had beaten Saracens 30–3 in the EDF Energy Cup semi-final shortly after our 2008 Grand Slam, one of my mates remarked on how well things were going for me personally, and Dean said, with his tongue in his cheek, 'It's only a matter of time before he hits a wall.'

A week later, we thrashed Ulster in a Magners League game, with me running in two tries. 'So when is he going to hit this wall?' my mate asked Dean.

'Bloody soon!' was his reply.

My mates are the same. They very rarely go over the top with any praise about my rugby to me. They're more keen to keep my feet firmly on the ground. 'Well done,' they'll say, 'but you messed up that move in the second half when you could have scored a try . . .' And, to be honest, that's the way I like it. I am one of them and always will be. I am where I am today because I got the breaks at the right time. I could so easily have had a life outside professional sport, as the story of my teenage years proves.

3

WHICH SHAPE BALL?

I CAN only remember playing mini-rugby a handful of times in primary school, and I certainly never got involved with any club. Even when I went to Amman Valley Comprehensive School, I spent most of my time playing for the second team because of the issue of my size. There were all kinds of county trials talked about all the time, and first- and second-team fixtures were seen as the be all and end all. But I never got a sniff of county recognition – and I honestly didn't want it anyway. I played for a laugh because my mates played, and to hell with Wales caps and all that business.

After a time, I lost interest in rugby. I only played very occasionally, and football came more into my life. I was a naturally left-sided player, and really enjoyed the game. And then there was gymnastics. I absolutely loved gymnastics.

I probably get my athleticism from my mother, who was a good sportswoman in her youth. It has to be her, because from what I have heard my father had no talent whatsoever in that area.

At comprehensive school, I was so hooked that I would spend every lunch hour in the gym. I credit gymnastics for a lot of the explosiveness and balance that I have on the rugby field nowadays, because it is a sport that demands that you constantly support your own body weight. I still see Dai Beynon, my old PE teacher, from time to time, and he always says that gymnastics got me where I am today.

I did floor routines, vaults over the horse and bench routines. I did gymnastics fairly seriously for about six years and got to a pretty decent standard. Of course, when you first start, you can get hurt, as I found out on plenty of occasions. I didn't help myself because my enthusiasm was such that I always wanted to be the one to try something new, and I ended up landing on my head quite a few times.

Despite my love of gymnastics, there were other sports I had no interest in whatsoever, such as athletics. Because I had pace, the teachers wanted me to do the 100 metres, but I just couldn't be bothered. The only thing I did get slightly into was the hurdles – there was a bit of a danger element to that – and I did that at county level. But, to me, there was nothing more boring than running around a track. It didn't seem like a challenge, and there was no risk, no danger element to it, as there was with gymnastics. The fact that I was able to do somersaults excited me, and I would even end up doing them on my own when I was down the park.

I can still do the sorts of flips you see the footballer Robert Earnshaw do after scoring a goal, because once you learn you never forget how; in fact, that is actually quite basic stuff. I've been asked by some of my friends to do a back somersault after scoring a try for Wales, but so far I've resisted the temptation. It's easy doing it in training, but, knowing my luck, if I tried it in front of thousands of people at the Millennium Stadium, it would be the one and only time I'd fall flat on my face.

I was criticised for theatrically diving up in the air while scoring a try for Wales in the loss to Fiji at the 2007 World Cup.

I remember Brynmor Williams was one observer who said that I shouldn't have done it under the circumstances. With respect, I think people such as Brynmor were reading far too much into it. I am a player who just loves scoring tries, and sometimes when you are scoring you are so pumped up you barely know what you are doing. The dive is just a sign of the pleasure I take from scoring.

After doing it in the Fiji game, I had so many kids come up to me in the weeks afterwards and talk excitedly about it. It felt good to have given them something to enjoy, and I have since thought, 'Why not?' If anyone is worried that I might drop the ball by diving up in the air, then I can assure them that when I cross the try line the ball is superglued to my hands.

Football has been my other love. I played a bit for the school and also for Cwmamman United juniors up through the age groups and then for the seniors when I was old enough. I don't want to sound cocky, but I found football far easier to play than rugby. I had a pal called Russell Gibbs, who has since moved to play semi-professional football in Australia, and together we banged in the goals for years.

I was a left-winger, and Russell was a striker, and we made a very good double act up front. Welsh League teams such as Afan Lido and Pontarddulais Town showed interest in us, and it got to the stage that Alan Curtis came to look at us on behalf of Swansea City. We would get thirty or forty goals each a season for Cwmamman in the Neath League, and after every match it was back to the clubhouse, where you would get five free pints if you'd scored a hat-trick. That meant Russell and I barely ever put our hands in our pockets for a post-match drink, but I wasn't there for the freebies. I went because all my mates were there, and the atmosphere was great. Yes, there were people there who took it more seriously, but to me it was only ever a game.

As for the Swansea City thing, well, it never came to me actually going to the club, but there was quite a serious interest. The guys at Cwmamman would tell me before games that Alan Curtis was there to watch me – at first I didn't even know who he was. But he came up to me after a game once and told me that Swansea were keeping an eye on me, to keep up the good form and that soon I would be invited to train with the club.

I played for Cwmamman against a Swansea City side once in a specially arranged game, and I impressed up against a defender called Keith Walker, who was at the club at the time. That led to more overtures from the Swans, but it wasn't the right time for me. And there was one thing that made it even more unlikely that it would go any further – Neath Rugby Club were interested in me.

Now, back then I was literally playing football one week for Cwmamman and rugby the next for Amman United, depending on which game took my fancy on a given weekend. I know it used to annoy a hell of a lot of people at both clubs, but my response was to tell them that I wasn't taking either sport seriously and just wanted to enjoy myself. The football club in particular took itself very seriously. You'd have sworn that they were in the Premiership judging by the attitude of some of them. I'm not criticising guys for caring. It was just that I had a completely different outlook.

I once missed a cup final for Cwmamman to play rugby for Amman United in a meaningless league game against Laugharne. We had beaten Laugharne by 60 points a few weeks earlier, but I opted for the rugby, as I knew it would be a nice open game in which I was likely to score a few tries. Cwmamman lost their final, but it genuinely didn't bother me. I loved playing both sports, and if I could get away with doing the same thing now, I probably would.

Alan Edmonds, who was coaching Amman United at the time, told me that a number of teams were interested in me. First up there was Neath – I spoke to Lyn Jones but was not offered anything concrete. Then Mike Ruddock, who was at Leinster at that time, showed interest, and there had also been an enquiry from a club called Blaydon, who were a feeder outfit for Newcastle in the English Premiership.

My thinking was that my best chance of being a professional sportsman was by playing rugby. I thought it would be easier to make the grade, and there was soon firmer interest being expressed by Blaydon, who told me that there would be a big opportunity to break into the Newcastle set-up if I did well with them.

So, on their invitation I went up there for a weekend, trained with them and played in a friendly match, doing very well. I liked the environment there and was chuffed to bits when they offered me the chance to go up and join them permanently. They were setting me up with a job, a car and a flat, and for a 19-year-old lad who had only ever known the Amman Valley it was a dazzling opportunity of a new life. I more or less had my bags packed ready to go.

But it wasn't cut and dried. At the time, I was working for the employment service, and it was a decent job that carried some prospects. So, it wasn't as if I had nothing whatsoever to stay for, and I did feel I was making a big decision. Then, just before I was due to go, Neath stepped in.

Ron Waldron, the former Wales coach, was still attached to Neath at the time, and he had come to watch me play for Amman United in our last game of the season. I had a terrible game and was red-carded towards the end for kicking someone in the head (it was not malicious). I knew Ron was there, and because of what happened I thought I had blown my chance, so I got used to the idea of going to Blaydon. I even had the finer details, including transport up there, all arranged.

But just days before I was due to set off, Lyn Jones rang my house. 'We'd like you to come and train with us,' he said. 'Come and spend the summer with us. We think you've got something.'

There was no promise of a long contract, but it was enough to persuade me not to go to Blaydon after all, even though I could have earned twice as much if I had upped sticks and left. It was a gamble, as Neath weren't going to pay me anything at first. But after training with them for the summer, they put me on something like £130 a week and threw in a car.

The car was the biggest heap of junk I had ever seen. It was a Fiesta, and it looked like it had been driven down an alley that was too narrow for it, with both sides of it scraped and caved in. But I didn't care. I didn't have another car at the time, and it would do for me. It was my first professional deal. Welcome to the big time.

I left sixth form early, before I had any idea that a life in professional sport lay ahead of me. I had been doing an advanced GNVQ (General National Vocational Qualification) in business studies and wasn't enjoying it. I loved school, but I wanted money in my pocket. My friends were going out at weekends, buying their first cars, and I was scratching by on what my mother could give me, which was hardly anything, considering she herself was struggling to make ends meet.

Mam didn't want me to leave, but I wanted my independence, and it wasn't as if I was doing A levels, either. I was never the brightest spark at school, but I was good at the hands-on subjects such as art, PE and technology. I have always been good at sketching, and when I was a kid I would often drift into my own little world, drawing things with a pencil. I used to doodle constantly. In the last couple of years, I have tried doing the odd oil painting, but since Georgie has come along I haven't had the time. I would like to go back to it in the future, though, because I do find it gives me a release, and I think we all need that in life.

Looking back, I wish I had worked harder in school, but when I left I didn't really stop to think, and I was ready to take whatever job came my way. The first one was with a local window firm. I had a mate, Ross, who was working there, and he told me that there was a position making and fitting windows. I was on about £30 a week, working my socks off. I was up and out of the house at 8 a.m. every morning. And sure enough, I was soon wondering why I had left school early.

I was treated like dirt and regarded by everyone as the company's dogsbody. I would make the tea and coffee, and I would be the one to go to the shop if someone wanted a sandwich. The shop was about three-quarters of a mile away, and sometimes I would come back with a sandwich for someone only for another guy to tell me that he wanted one too and to go back again.

Not only that, but I was put through the long-weight (wait) and tartan-paint routines by the guys, who clearly thought I was put on the earth for their amusement. We were based on an industrial estate, and during the first week I was there one of the blokes turned to me and said, 'Go across the road to the carpenter's and see if he has any of those long weights.'

'Sure, no problem,' I said, eager to be helpful, and off I went in search of a long weight.

'Stay there, and I'll go get one,' they said at the carpenter's, immediately cottoning onto the fact that I was the victim of a classic practical joke. Soon enough, I started wondering where they were with my long weight.

I was naive and nervous, and used to get caught out all the time. The tartan-paint joke was a case in point. I obviously knew what tartan looked like, but the penny didn't drop, and when I innocently went and asked one of the painters on site for it, he looked at me and said with disgust, 'Are you stupid?'

There were other jobs I went on to do that were the pits, but perhaps they gave me an insight into the real world. I worked at a bakery for a time, before being laid off. I enjoyed that job. It was a factory bakery run by a firm called Morris Brothers in Llandybie. There were good parts about it, such as the fact that I was working with my mates and we had some great banter. But it was never as if I wanted to stay long term. I was just there to do the menial stuff: lifting, fetching, carrying, stacking bread and making up bases for cakes, which was easily done just by loading a machine. It was boring, and I was eventually let go. I didn't blame the firm. If I had owned that bakery, I wouldn't have employed me, because I spent a lot of the time just walking around the place, usually like a zombie as a result of the early starts we had. But that didn't mean I wasn't gutted when they told me I was going, because it was money in my pocket, after all, and jobs could be quite difficult to come by at that time.

I spent a little time on the dole, and I also worked now and then on local building sites, labouring, lugging breeze-blocks and mixing cement, but that situation didn't last long. On one of my frequent visits to the job centre, I noticed that there was a youth-training scheme on offer, involving working in the job centre itself. It only paid about £35 to £40 a week, but I looked around, and it seemed a decent place to be. I knew that if nothing else it would be a chance to help people and do something much more worthwhile. It had to be better than putting a window together or making an egg-custard tart. Here was something that was likely to give me a sense of accomplishment at the end of each day.

So I went for it and got it – and it proved to be a real success. I had found something I was good at: dealing with unemployed people and helping them to find work. I was even promoted and told by the managers that I had a genuine flair for the work.

I loved it. I started off doing paperwork behind the scenes, but before long I was put on the front line, meeting and interviewing people and placing them in positions. They produced statistics that revealed just how good you were at placing people, and I was always top or thereabouts. I found the work challenging and rewarding, and I had gone from wearing an apron or scruffy jeans covered in dirt, to wearing trousers and a shirt and tie in a proper office environment. I felt like I was getting somewhere at last, and I would even have people come in with thank-you cards for me after I had placed them in a job that they were enjoying. That felt bloody good.

I can still remember the different types of people who used to come in. There were the ones who were genuinely looking for work and would come in and apply for loads of things. Then you would have those who you knew were working while still claiming and actually didn't want you to find them a job. Finally, there were those who had been signing on for years, who had no interest in work and would come in and answer my questions with a total lack of interest. A couple of times, I managed to get people into work who had been on the dole for about five years, and it was a massive boost – something to show for what you were doing day in, day out.

Don't get me wrong, I wouldn't swap what I do now for the world, but there are times I find myself wondering how far I could have gone in that line of work had my opportunity to earn a living in rugby not come along. What I do know is that if the rugby hadn't worked out, I would have been applying to go back there. I'd found something that I was good at, and my results showed as much. I was well thought of by my bosses, and the fact that I could speak English and Welsh was another massive thing in my favour.

After a while, I was asked to take newcomers to the office under my wing and train them, and I got a massive kick out of doing that as well. It did wonders for my self-esteem, having thought just a short time before that I was only good enough to be a dogsbody at a window firm. Before I worked at the job centre, I used to drift off when people explained things to me. Information would go in one ear and out the other. But at the employment service I really took on board every piece of advice I was given.

I well remember the training we were given in how to deal with awkward customers – training that I found you definitely needed. In my time there, I had people shouting at me and being abusive. There were times when you would key a bloke's name into the computer and a message would come up on screen, saying 'Potentially physical!' That was never what you wanted to see, but you learned how to deal with it, how to adjust your behaviour accordingly.

I liked the fact that every day was different. On Monday, you might get five people into placements; on Tuesday, you might draw a complete blank.

My mates would sometimes come in, and they would ask for me to deal with them, but I knew that they were hobbling so wanted to avoid them. We would sit down, and I would say with a smile on my face, 'I know you are working, so don't give me any bullshit.'

'Yeah, OK. I'll stop, I'll stop,' they would say.

I also had a great relationship with the people I worked with. Some of the women were like mother figures to me, and I still see them around town every now and again.

At the end of the day, I think you instinctively know when you are good at something – when you have found something you are suited to and can thrive at. Then life is good. I've heard it said that if you enjoy what you do for a living, you don't actually do a day's work in your entire life. I think there's definitely something in that.

Luckily that definitely rings true for me today. However, just like in any profession, I had to work my way up in rugby, and my early days with Neath were far from glamorous. We would train in the morning, whether it be a skills session or weights, and in the afternoon I would have to go and see Roy the groundsman, who would give me jobs to do. It could be painting a wall, marking the pitch out, tidying the stands and terraces, or collecting rubbish. If I had a spare hour, I would go out on the pitch and practise my passing, because I joined Neath as a scrum-half at first. Sometimes we would train late in the afternoons as well, and it was quite demanding, but I knuckled down because I wanted to play for Neath.

The difficulty was that this came after I had worked at the employment service, and going back to doing menial jobs such as collecting rubbish was tough to take. There were times when I felt I had taken a step backwards. Saying that, though, I suppose I always knew that there was a high reward at the end if I put my heart and soul into Neath.

I followed that routine for most of the first season, but when a few injuries started to kick in I found myself with opportunities to go along with the first team. My first full league match was against Pontypridd at Sardis Road in a match that was live on television. I was 11 stone soaking wet, and the first time the ball came my way I was short-armed – not deliberately – by Dale McIntosh, Ponty's giant back-row man. Bang! My nose was broken. When my head cleared, I thought, 'I can't do this. I can't cope with all this.' While I have never been afraid of going up against bigger guys, I must admit that the level of physicality that day shocked me. It was a real wake-up call, showing me what I was going to have to get used to.

But I played on. I knew I had to. If I had gone off then, it would have been the end of me. And things improved. We lost the game quite convincingly – Ponty were very strong at the time – but I made a couple of late breaks and had a few nice runs, which gave me some positives to take away.

I was back on the fringes of the team for a long time after that, getting on the bench a couple of times and making a few substitute appearances. I wasn't unhappy with that, because I knew I still had things to learn and had to bide my time. Then a Heineken Cup game away to Perpignan came along. Patrick Horgan, our number-one scrum-half, had to pull out and I was asked to travel. I was grateful for that, but things took another twist the night before the match when I was told I would be starting. To say I was nervous would be an understatement. Perpignan were a great side – they still are – and at home in their Stade Aimé Giral fortress they were all but unbeatable.

What an experience that match was for me. We were stuffed by 40 points, and when they scored in virtually the first minute, I remember thinking to myself, 'Shane, you're out of your depth here.' But it didn't really turn out like that. Although we were hammered, it went quite well for me personally. I made a couple of breaks and did a few things that I was pleased with. However, nothing could have prepared me for what happened after the match.

No sooner had I showered and changed than the Perpignan chairman was coming up to me and asking me to sign there and then for his club. I must have made quite an impression on him. I was shocked and didn't have a clue how to deal with such a situation. All I could do was go running to Lyn like a little kid and tell him what had happened. Lyn went and spoke to him, and when he came back he told me that Perpignan were offering Neath a fee of about £15,000 for me to join them. I just thought the whole thing was crazy. There I was having just played only my second full game for Neath, and my first in the Heineken Cup, and I was being offered the chance to go and play for one of the great clubs in Europe. Of course, I did not end up making the switch, but the episode did have an impact on my career.

At the time, I was still being paid weekly, but after that I signed a proper contract with Neath. The Perpignan interest ended up being a good bargaining tool, and while the money I was on with Neath wasn't great, it was at least a proper one-year deal that gave me some security. For the first time, I felt like a proper professional player. Neath would be the club where I would make my name.

4

THOSE GNOLL DAYS

ONCE NEATH, always Neath. The club that gave me my big chance in rugby might not exist in its old form these days, but it will always be my club, and it will always have a place in my heart.

Top-level rugby in Wales has long since gone through its regional revolution, with clubs such as Neath now competing in the semi-professional Welsh Premiership. It's a decent enough league, but everyone knows it's nothing like it used to be. The Welsh All Blacks, aka Neath, are now the dominant force at that level and were champions again last season.

None of these changes alter the allegiance I feel to the Gnoll, mind you. There has always been a huge sense of belonging at Neath, a bit of a 'no-one likes us, we don't care' motto underpinning the whole club. There's little doubt that Neath are one of the great club sides in the history of the Welsh game and probably one of the most successful. The great players who have donned the famous jersey are too numerous to mention. But in my time there, while we were always a threat to the best clubs in Wales, while we were always there or thereabouts, we never quite managed to bring home any silverware.

The closest we came was the Welsh Cup final in 2001 when

we lost 13–8 to Newport. But I'd hardly call that match a classic moment in my career. I remember it was the last game Gary Teichmann played for the Black and Ambers, and as their squad was so expensively assembled, the pressure was really on them to deliver that day.

They did, but only just. Shane Howarth was the key for them, controlling the match in the second half with some intelligent tactical kicking, but it could have been different for us had the referee awarded a try when I ran onto a chip by Rowland Phillips and dived on the ball at the same time as Shane. Referee Clayton Thomas decided I had been beaten to the ball by Shane, but, suffice to say, I thought differently – and television replays seemed to side with me. But it was to no avail. Our wing Kevin James got a late try to give us a ray of hope, but Newport were powerful at the time and did what they had to do to hold out.

There was also the Celtic Cup final of February 2003, when we went to the Millennium Stadium to face Munster, but once again we had to be content with being runners-up in a tournament that ran alongside the old Welsh Premiership. Again, I wouldn't class it as a red-letter day in my career. The competition was very much an 'after the Lord Mayor's show' sort of affair in comparison to the Heineken Cup, but, regardless, we were no match for a Munster side who were beginning to forge a reputation as one of the true powerhouses of the European game.

Rightly or wrongly, the Irish provinces have a reputation for not going full-pelt at anything outside of the Heineken Cup, but when there's a trophy at stake, as there was that day, you can count on them to come out firing. We had conceded four penalties to Ronan O'Gara before we knew where we were. Our discipline was just shocking. Lee Jarvis kept us in touch with a few penalties and a drop goal, but Munster then ran in three tries through Marcus Horan, Alan Quinlan and Rob Henderson, and their fans were in full song with their 'Fields of Athenry' anthem long before the final whistle. We had the last word with a try from our prop, Adam Jones, in injury time, but we were well beaten – and we knew it.

And that was typical of us. We had some good players, but in my time at the Gnoll we never were able to really deliver as a team when it mattered most. We were always knocking on the door but never good enough to break it down. We never really fulfilled our potential.

However, I cannot recall a time when I wanted to leave the club. I was ambitious to be successful, of course I was, but to me what mattered most was enjoying the game and enjoying the style of rugby that Neath played, and I could always say that was the case at the Gnoll. I was playing rugby for the love of it – that's still true to a fair extent now – and I saw playing regularly for Neath as enough of an achievement. I was always so preoccupied with staying in the first team, and I never once would have believed that I would make the Wales team after just a season and a half of playing for Neath. Yet my rise at the club was not an ordinary one.

As I've mentioned, I joined the club as a scrum-half, having played on the wing only a handful of times before. But scrum-half is a tough position to play, especially when you have come from a club in the lower divisions – and don't forget, that's where I had been with Amman United. As a scrum-half, you are absolutely pivotal to the direction of the team. You are very much a decision maker who is right in the mix, with the rest of the team looking to you to orchestrate things. I struggled with this responsibility. Even though you see more of the ball at half-back, there is far less margin for error.

I was on the bench as a substitute scrum-half during a cup game against Wrexham in December 1998 when a sequence of injuries meant that we needed a wing to go on. Lyn Jones asked if I fancied it, and as I just wanted to get on the field I said yes. I discovered that I really enjoyed it. I loved the extra freedom and found I had more space to play in and express myself. Lyn noticed how well I had taken to the position and asked me if I would like a run of games there. From then on, I never looked back. It did take me a while to get completely comfortable on the wing, but I seemed to get better with every game, and I certainly enjoyed it more than playing at number 9.

At scrum-half, you are there to feed the back line or the forwards, but on the wing it is about taking on opponents and testing your skill and speed, and that gave me a real buzz. On the wing, I found that I was getting 40 yards of field in which to run at people, and I was scoring tries, whereas at scrum-half all I could remember was having my fingers stood on in a ruck. I began to love playing on the wing, and before long it was the only position for me.

The odd jobs I did as a new apprentice at Neath came to an end about a year and a half after I joined them. I just started going home instead of going to see Roy. I don't know whether I was officially allowed to or not – it just came about naturally as I began to play more and more games and to behave more like an experienced professional player. I'd still help Roy now if he needed a hand, but times were changing back then.

At the start of my time with Neath, I didn't feel as though I fitted in. After a while, though, I realised that I had as much right as anyone to be there, and I started to take myself more seriously as a professional rugby player. I began training on my own in addition to what I was doing at the club. I also curtailed what I drank and tried to eat the right things.

When I joined Neath, there were already guys there whom I knew, people such as Leighton Gerrard, Geraint Evans and

Delme Williams, who were all from my area. Delme, who was in my class at school, was a good wing himself and was tipped for big things at the same time that I was starting to emerge, but he had a serious knee injury. He then went off to Llanelli and was never quite the same player. Saying that, he had bags of potential and with a bit more luck could have gone on to higher things.

Those guys helped me settle in, and believe me there were times when you needed a few allies in those days. At Neath, there was a more experienced section of the squad, blokes such as Leighton, Geraint, Rowland Phillips, Andrew Millward, James Storey, Robin Jones, Pat Horgan and Scott Eggar – who I thought was a total nutcase – to name but a few. On away trips, we always played drinking games on the bus on the way home, and boys would be throwing up left, right and centre. Even though we were professional by then, that was one part of the amateur era that seemed to survive for a spell. It used to be carnage at times, but while the more experienced lads had been doing it for ages, the youngsters didn't know what had hit them.

At one time, it seemed like I was copping it on every away trip. We would have to do forfeits, drinking yards of ale and funnels of beer, and there was no question of getting out of it by being sick, because if you were sick you had to be sick into your own glass, and then you were made to drink the contents.

I wasn't too bad on the yard of ale, as I had had some practice in my youth days at Amman United. However, the pressure was still on, because you wanted to impress the more experienced lads who called the shots. This sort of thing is almost unheard of in the professional game today, but back then I suppose it was one way to earn a few stripes in the eyes of the more senior boys, and I felt it did that for me.

When I was 'initiated' at Neath, I was slightly fortunate, as I was one of about 15 others whose turn it was to go through the ritual on that particular day. It was after a European Shield match against Padova in October 1998. We'd lost 28–17, but that didn't mean we got out of it. We were made to strip naked on the bus and were blindfolded before having the living daylights beaten out of us by the old heads in the side. That wasn't the end of it, though. We were then made to drink all manner of concoctions and eat things such as chillies. We were also made to crawl down the aisle of the bus with the seat covers pulled over our heads, and on our way we were whipped with belts and beaten with sticks.

Then it was time for a game of 'Kiss the Turd'. This involved dipping your head – still blindfolded – into a bucket and kissing whatever was in there. I would like to think that it wasn't actually what was in the title of the game, but to this day I don't know – and I don't really want to know. Believe me, compared to some of the initiations I've heard about at other clubs, that one was probably quite tame. Times change, though, and I know we certainly wouldn't get away with anything like that these days at the Ospreys.

Having said that, it's experiences such as those – you have to go through them to fully understand them – that help you forge a feeling for a badge. Neath is the sort of club that gets under your skin if you play for them for a decent length of time. You develop a sense of belonging, a sense of being part of the family, and that never really leaves you. Some of my best rugby was played in a Neath shirt, and I will never forget that. I owe the club a lot, and I am very conscious of the fact that I would not have got where I have in the game had it not been for them.

I still look out for their results every weekend, and I was chuffed that my testimonial game at the Millennium Stadium this year was part of the same event as the Welsh Cup final that saw Neath beat Pontypridd. It was brilliant to see them win a trophy, especially as I am still friendly with quite a few of the boys who play for the team, and it rounded off a fantastic day for me.

I don't know this for sure, but I always felt that when I played for Neath we were a side that teams hated losing to more than others. And with Neath, you always had the Gnoll factor to take into account. Even the name of the place suggests something different is in store, something unique, and while I know there are plenty of grounds in British rugby that would lay claim to having a special atmosphere, there was definitely something about our little home ground. With one side of it completely open to the cricket pitch – save for the temporary seating that was put up from time to time – you wouldn't mark it down as one of those intimidating enclosed venues. But there was just something about it that always made it a tough place for visiting teams to come to and a place that stoked the fire in your belly if you were donning the black jersey.

I know that's what it always used to do for me. There were times I was petrified playing there, because the home supporters were the kind who would let you know about it if you were playing poorly.

In one match against Newport, not long after I had been dropped from the Wales team in 2001, I had a terrible night. I was playing too soon, having had a nasty injury to my elbow caused by a bike fall. For some reason, I was taking the kicks at goal that night, and I missed about the first three attempts I had. I then made a chip kick that went straight into a pair of Newport hands and resulted in a try being scored against us. To cap it all, Jason Forster, their burly openside flanker, then put in a big hit on me, and the skin graft on my elbow was torn. I had to come off. The wound needed about 20 stitches, and as I trooped off I remember thinking that it was the worst match of my entire life.

But that was a low point of my career. There was another time when I scored a hat-trick of tries against the Black and Ambers, and in another encounter, against Cardiff, who we were always desperate to put one over on, I claimed another three tries. A few people later told me that it was the best treble they had seen scored at the ground, which was nice.

So, there were highs and lows for me at my home ground, though a great atmosphere was always guaranteed. And I suppose that's the key to the Gnoll – the place was what the fans made it. While there were usually only a couple of thousand there, you felt the crowd's passion for the game and for their team like nowhere else. They used to make the noise of a crowd double their size, and there were games when I felt like I was playing at a much bigger ground.

Match days at the Gnoll will stay with me for ever, but so will the people at Neath who influenced me most, and there is probably nobody who has done so more than Lyn Jones, the man who coached me for a decade and more. In fact, he coached me for my entire professional career up until he left the Ospreys.

Everyone has an opinion about Lyn. He is not what you would call one of the game's more conventional characters. But he is no mug, and I owe him a hell of a lot. To put it bluntly, Lyn is mad, as mad as they come. But I have got used to his ways down the years – and I have enormous personal and professional respect for him.

When I first started playing for Neath, he called me over once during a training session for a word about tactics. While we were stood talking, Lyn unzipped his tracksuit bottoms and started peeing, there and then, while continuing the conversation as if what he was doing was as normal as eating an apple. This was before I was used to him, and to be honest I could hardly believe that this bloke was the coach of Neath and was doing things like that.

At other times, I'd see him doing interviews for television. He'd be standing there talking with a straight face to the reporter, all the while with his trousers around his ankles. Lyn might not have been a media expert, but he did know that they were only going to film his top half.

The first time I went to meet Lyn at his office at the Gnoll, one of the first things he said to me was, 'How big's your cock?' I was dumbfounded. In my youthful naivety, I remember wondering, 'Is he serious, semi-serious or just totally winding me up? Do I answer him or just pretend I never heard the question?' What made it worse was that he asked the question with a completely deadpan look on his face and probably took joy from seeing how petrified I was of him. I was nervous enough as a hopeful kid going to meet the Neath head coach, but this really had me squirming. I can't recall if I ever answered his question. He probably jumped in and helped me out as my jaw hit the floor.

For a long time, I didn't know how to take Lyn. I used to look at him and think, 'This is the guy in charge of our careers.' He didn't mess around with me as much in later years, probably because he knew I had worked him out, or perhaps he mellowed with age.

It didn't take me long to realise that there is much more to Lyn than playing the fool. For one, he has a marvellously innovative rugby brain. Lyn has come up with game plans and tactics through the seasons that I have never encountered before, and, I'll tell you what, almost all of them have worked. He is a unique character – one of the strangest people I have ever met – but he knows the game, and he almost always knows what works and what doesn't. Sometimes we did moves on the training ground that seemed crazy, and you knew that only Lyn Jones could have come up with them, but I guess that kind of thing became the norm for me.

I don't think that you can question his coaching ability. His man-management is a bit off the wall, but he is a very good strategist. He has a barrel of knowledge and isn't afraid to seek the opinions of his players. He would ask us whether we thought his plans were going to work and was willing to take on board suggestions.

Mike Cuddy, the chairman of the Ospreys, and before that Neath, is another guy who has had a major impact on my career. I got to know him early on, as he was always the one who put the contracts on the table. He helped me out a lot in my early days and was the one who sorted me out with that clapped-out Fiesta, which at least saved my mother from having to take me back and forth to training. But he's done so much more since. When I bought my first house, for example, there was a lot of work that needed doing to it construction-wise, and he sent a few of the boys who work for him around to help out. Mike's always been the person I have gone to if I needed help with anything. He's been a bit of a father figure to me, and I have always gone to him with any rugby-related problems. But he also came to my rescue when I was thrown in a prison cell in Cyprus – of which more later – and I couldn't think of who else to turn to, sending out a solicitor, John Morris, at the drop of a hat. The only thing Mike has ever wanted from me in return is performances on the field, and I have certainly tried to repay him for his kindness in that way.

There are others: Steve Richards, the physio, known as 'Rittaz' to the boys, for one. I have worked with him countless times when I have been injured. He has been a huge help to me, teaching me different ways of getting fit, and I won't forget that.

But, as I say, it was a family at Neath, as it is now with the Ospreys. There are so many people who have made my life more enjoyable. I cannot think of anyone I have ever really had a problem with. And maybe it was because I was so happy that I was able to fulfil my potential as a rugby player, as it wasn't long after I made the breakthrough in the black jersey that Wales came calling – or, I should say, a certain Mr Henry.

5

WALES EXPECTS

IF SOMEONE had told me when I signed my first contract with Neath that I would be in the Wales team within 18 months, I would have dismissed them as being wildly optimistic. It was just something that I never envisaged happening so quickly, especially as I wasn't even sure whether I would be good enough to get a regular place in the Neath team. But that was what happened. As the 1999 World Cup finished – a tournament I watched with the fans, cheering Wales on in pubs – and the 2000 Six Nations approached, there I was, little Shane Williams from the Amman Valley, being talked about as a contender for the Wales team, even though I was barely 21.

I remember after one run of good games for Neath, a couple of people approached me and spoke about the possibility of a call-up to the Under-21 squad. That alone excited me hugely, though I never did play for the age-group side. That was probably due to the way I came through into the professional ranks. I was unknown right up into my late teens, and by the time I was being touted for the Under-21s I was more or less too old.

But all this complimentary talk got me thinking that I must be doing something right. The 1999–2000 season was my second full campaign, and by then I couldn't help but notice my name appearing more and more in the papers. When that first happens to a player, I don't care who they are, they will be chuffed. I know I was, and I was even more pleased when I saw a programme on the television after a game one weekend, which saw Lyn Jones being interviewed by Nigel Walker, the ex-Wales wing who now works for the BBC. Nigel mentioned to Lyn that I was being talked about more and more, and Lyn responded by saying that I was a special player and that it was only a matter of time before I played for Wales. Well, to hear a remark like that sent my confidence soaring into orbit. It was the first time I was aware of being talked about on TV, and I can't really describe how it felt. And the way the media works, it just triggered more and more attention for me, more and more debate about whether I was ready to be called up to the Test scene. Needless to say, it was all fine by me.

I slowly got used to seeing myself scoring tries on television and began for the first time to believe that, yes, I might well be ready to go to the next level. Why not? Throughout my first year at Neath, I had been anonymous, going through the motions. Now I was starting to analyse different aspects of my game, becoming more self-critical in the way a professional should be.

I was starting to believe that I was playing better than the people in my position who were already in the Wales set-up. Gareth Thomas and Dafydd James were about at the time, as was Wayne Proctor. Gareth and Dafydd were obviously different types of players from me altogether, and their presence naturally prompted some people to say that I was too small to play for Wales. I, of course, thought differently, but thinking back they were probably right: I was only 11 stone. Then again, I was more concerned with how I was playing for my club and couldn't see too many others doing better than me. Maybe I was being a bit naive, but soon enough it was time for the conjecture to stop.

Graham Henry had organised a trial match immediately before the 2000 Six Nations at St Helen's, a sort of throwback to the old Probables–Possibles face-offs. There was no phone call from the Wales management. The first I heard of it was when my grandmother called me to say that she had bought a paper and that I was in the Probables team to play for Wales. 'You're going to play for Wales in the Six Nations,' she cooed.

'Calm down,' I said. 'It doesn't work like that.' But while I was trying to be nonchalant about it all, deep down I was incredibly excited. I genuinely didn't expect to play in the 2000 Six Nations, but I did think to myself, 'You never know . . .'

The day of the trial arrived, and it was a strange sort of atmosphere. There were a lot of players gathered together at St Helen's, and I remember looking at the ones who were far more experienced than I was and thinking that they must be more nervous than me. The butterflies in my stomach weren't that bad. I had no real immediate expectations so told myself to just go out and enjoy it. While I didn't see much of the ball early on, I had a few runs later and came off thinking that while I hadn't been outstanding by any means, I had certainly done myself no harm in the long run.

We got showered and headed across to the Swansea clubhouse, which overlooks the field and the beach, for some food. At that stage, the most I expected was to make the Wales A squad, which was also being picked. But when Graham Henry came in with his list and read out the A squad, I wasn't included. I was disappointed but told myself that I had plenty of time to make my mark and to put the whole afternoon down to experience.

When the second list was read out, the senior squad, I actually switched off, so low was my expectation of being named. I took no notice at all and just got stuck into my food. The next thing I knew, people were coming up to me and saying congratulations. I realised that I had made the full Wales squad, although I hadn't heard my name being called out. I was just amazed, and at the same time my stomach was churning with excitement. I could scarcely believe it, because while I had played reasonably well, I didn't think I had pulled up any trees, and that is what I thought I needed to do to stand a realistic chance of selection.

But I had obviously started a lot further down the road than I had imagined. Henry's opinion of me going into the afternoon must have been better than I could possibly have hoped for. So, two weeks before the championship opener at home to France, I met up with the rest of the Wales squad at the Vale of Glamorgan Hotel. My whole family was naturally elated, but so was Gail's family. She was my girlfriend at that time, and her grandparents even threw a party for me. Since then, Gail's granddad, John Price, has been one of my biggest supporters.

I remember being an hour late for the first meeting. I'd gone back to my room, and unbeknown to me the get-together had been brought forward. I walked into the meeting room and was horrified to discover my lateness, but I got away with it, and I have to say that Graham Henry was great with me – he was like a great-uncle to me. However, I felt like a little kid among grown-ups: completely lost and out of my depth. As far as I was concerned, I didn't belong in this company, and I was paranoid about what the others thought of me. I imagined them laughing at me behind my back and saying who the hell is this kid coming in here looking like a little schoolboy. I now don't for a moment think they thought that, but at the time it was different.

I was sharing rooms with people such as Rob Howley and Allan Bateman, not just established internationals, but British Lions. They were nice as pie, but I could not help but feel very intimidated by them. And then there was Henry himself – he scared the living daylights out of me. You have to remember that at the time he was on a real high with the Wales team. There was very much a feeling in Wales, never mind just amongst the team, that he could do no wrong and that whatever he said went. He was even christened the 'Great Redeemer' at one stage, which had religious groups up in arms, but that was an indication of how revered he was by most of the media and public.

It took a long time for me to get over my awkwardness and the fears that I had. Back then, we used to stay in camp for a long time, but I used to spend most of the time we weren't training cooped up in my room. If the boys went for a coffee, I would slip away to be on my own, because I just felt so out of place. The lads tried to get me involved, but I just couldn't get over my feelings of inadequacy. I couldn't come to terms with the fact that I was a working-class kid from the Amman Valley who was now in a four-star hotel with the Wales team and able to order anything I liked from room service whenever I wanted it. I was just so unnerved.

In training, there were all manner of moves and calls, which all the experienced players knew off by heart but which were alien to me, and I felt I would never pick them up, that I'd never fit in. Neil Jenkins in particular went out of his way to help me – you won't meet a nicer bloke in the game – trying to get me involved as much as he could and imploring me not to worry so much about things. 'We've all been there,' he would say. He had played for Wales at an even younger age than I had, and he insisted that he had been the same when he was first called up.

I guess my shyness was holding me back. It was very much my own problem, to do with how reserved I was as a person at the time. The fact that it took me about two or three years to be comfortable with being seen as a Wales international rugby player says it all. Being part of the Six Nations squad was one thing, but being part of the team was quite another.

Surely I wasn't going to win selection for the opening game against France?

I was grappling with a number of fears at the time: what if I had to play in front of all those people at the Millennium Stadium? What if I didn't get picked? What would people think of me then? What did the other players really think of me? What if the coaches had made a major mistake in picking me?

So when I was named on the bench to face the French, it came as a relief to me. It was the best of both worlds: I wasn't playing from the start, so I didn't have to cope with all the pressure that that would have brought, but I hadn't been ignored altogether, so I didn't have to feel like I'd let anyone down. I secretly hoped, too, that I wouldn't be put on during the game. That way there was no chance I could do anything wrong.

As it turned out, I got 25 minutes, and to this day people say that when I walked to the white line to join the fray, I looked like I was going to face a firing squad. I was absolutely beside myself with fear. I remember the physio Mark Davies calling over to me and saying, 'Shane, warm up.' I was almost paralysed with apprehension and decided to pretend that I hadn't heard him. But then the call went up again even louder, and I knew that there was no getting out of it. I can honestly say that I didn't want to go on and make my debut for Wales.

At that stage, we were about 20 points behind. I was in such a daze that I wasn't even aware of the score, but I knew it was turning sour for us, and now these people wanted to put me on in direct opposition to Émile N'Tamack, France's talisman at the time. He was one of the best wingers who had ever played for France, and there I was being sent into the lion's den to face him. My heart just sank.

But – and I know a lot of players talk about how their feelings change when they take the field – my fears washed away from me as I ran on to take my place on the wing for Wales. I just suddenly vowed to give it my best shot and to hell with whether I was actually proved good enough. 'Just give me that bloody ball,' I whispered under my breath. 'Whether I'm good or bad, I don't care any more.'

How did it go? Well, in terms of my overall contribution, not bad at all. I did most of the basics well, and I was lively and at least looked dangerous in the short time that I was on the field. But, unfortunately, a lot of that good work was undone by one incident.

Not long after I'd run on, I made a half-break. I thought I was going to get through and make some really great yardage, but I was hauled down by one of their defenders. As I released the ball out of the tackle, I could see N'Tamack looming into the space where I'd flipped up the ball. I swear that he had a smile on his face as he intercepted my offload and galloped 40 yards down the other end of the field to score.

I wanted to die there and then. It's almost impossible to describe how it feels to make such an obvious blunder in the glare of so many thousands of your fellow countrymen and women, all of whom are desperate to see their team win. For a split second, you feel a bit like you've murdered someone. I probably looked as though I was going to cry, but, fair play to them, quite a few of the lads, in particular Dai Young, the captain, made a point of coming up to me and saying not to worry about it.

I listened to their encouragement and remember thinking, 'Shane, if you just curl up and die now, then you are never going to do this again.' So I did the opposite. I went out and tried to express myself after that, putting the N'Tamack incident to the back of my mind as best I could – and I got into the game and enjoyed it.

It was difficult to blot out that one pass and interception, but by the end of the match I had had a go, and I knew it. I had got my hands on the ball, darted around a little bit and given the French defence something to think about at times. OK, I had not scored a spectacular try, and we had at the end of the day lost 36–3, but one thing at a time, I thought.

What's more, I had at least given my teammates something to laugh about with the size of my shirt. Unlike the tight fits of the modern era, I swear I had been given one of Dai Young's shirts to wear that day. It was like a tent on me, and there was no end of piss-taking about it. But I loved that, because all of a sudden I began to feel part of the group.

I was also teased about my N'Tamack mistake: 'You've had it now. You're dropped for Italy next week.' But the guys had their tongues firmly in their cheeks. I knew that there were indeed no guarantees, but at least I was starting to warm to this Wales thing, instead of feeling like an outcast.

There was a black-tie dinner at the stadium that night, and as Richard Smith, the scrum-half who was at Ebbw Vale at the time, and I were the new caps, everyone toasted their drinks to us. Even though we had lost, the atmosphere wasn't that bad. The attitude among the boys was, 'Let's get over this quickly and bounce back.'

I enjoyed that evening, and I savoured the feeling that whatever happened from then on, nobody could ever take my cap away from me. I had a few drinks and kept going up to Graham Henry and saying, 'Sorry about that pass today.' I must have said it ten times. He was probably sick of the sight of me by the end of the night, but he didn't show it if he was. I think he sensed that I was on a high and that the relief of having got my debut out of the way was flooding out of me. 'Don't worry,' he told me. 'Worse things than that will happen in your career.'

I took those words on board, and they acted as a kick up the backside. I needed to stop worrying so much about everything. The whole Wales experience up to that point had seen me racked with fear. While nerves were, to a certain extent, understandable, I had taken it to the extreme, going way over the top and building things up into problems that shouldn't have existed. But now I figured that if I could get through the experience at a full Millennium Stadium of making a mistake that had led to an opposition try, I could tackle anything.

I have made a lot of mistakes in my career since, but I have not gone into a corner and cried about any of them – and it's that experience during my first cap that I have used as a benchmark. France 2000 was a watershed for Shane Williams.

While I thought that I had done reasonably well, others whose opinion I respected seemed to confirm as much. The French full-back Thomas Castaignède talked about how he thought I had a great future, while Henry underlined that he thought I had done well when I came on.

I suspected that they might just be being kind to me, but then I was blown away when I was actually picked to start the next game, against Italy, instead of Dafydd James. While Italy are a team that has very much improved since joining the old Five Nations to make it the Six Nations, they were not France, and here was a chance for me really to show what I could do.

It was tight early on, with Neil Jenkins and Diego Domínguez trading penalties, but shortly before half-time my big moment arrived: my first try for Wales. I remember the pass coming from Mark Taylor in the centre after we had stretched their defence with a flowing movement. It was one of those situations all wingers dream of. You know you are going to score the moment you catch the ball, and planting it on the deck was a fantastic feeling. We soared to a 30–9 lead by the interval, and the day ended with an emphatic 47–16 victory, which could have been even more convincing had we not gone to sleep for a period in the second half.

But if I was on a high after the Italy game, I was about to be handed a harsh lesson in just how tough international rugby at Test level could be as we headed to Twickenham to face an England team very much on the up. Under Clive Woodward, they were on fire and very much building towards their 2003 World Cup triumph. It had been so long since we had been to Twickenham and won that it was starting to become a real hoodoo, although we had beaten them at Wembley the year before. That probably didn't help us, because I sensed that the English were out for revenge for what had happened that day underneath the twin towers when Scott Gibbs had danced through right at the death for a try that denied the old enemy the Grand Slam.

We matched them on the scoreboard for half an hour in 2000, with Jenks swapping penalties with Jonny Wilkinson, but when their hooker, Phil Greening, streaked away for a try around the half-hour mark, it all went despairingly downhill.

With both Quinnell brothers, Scott and Craig, being sin-binned, it was up front where we were really taken to task, and it was no surprise that England's famous back-row trio of Richard Hill, Neil Back and Lawrence Dallaglio all got second-half tries, with Dallaglio carrying half our team over with him when he crossed late on.

It was an eye-opener for me, another step up from what I had been through in the first two matches. I remember taking a couple of hits in the first half and noticing straight away that this was a level of physicality that I had never encountered before. It was as if every time I was touched by a white shirt, I got hurt. From Neath to Wales had been one massive step up – this was another.

I was up against Austin Healey that day, as busy a player as I had ever faced. He wasn't short of a word or two of advice, either, and kept piping up with, 'Where's your gas, Shane? Where's your gas?' I'd been warned that Healey was 'chopsy' before the game, but this was another area in which I didn't have much experience. Realising that I was out of my depth in the verbal exchanges, I let him have his say without firing anything much back. In any case, it's hard to compete in those stakes when you are part of a team that is getting such a hiding.

By the end of the match, I didn't think that I had played that badly, but there was another little sideshow involving me that was about to erupt. In the post-match press conference, their wing, Ben Cohen, was asked by a couple of Welsh reporters for a verdict on 'Shane's contribution'. In reply, he supposedly asked, 'Shane who?' Now, Ben has since said that he was trying to ascertain whether the questioner meant me or Shane Howarth, but our media, not to mention most of the rest of the Welsh rugby public, took it as arrogance – as if he was questioning my right to be on the same pitch – and a sign of disrespect towards one of their own from an Englishman looking to rub Welsh noses in it after a heavy defeat.

I am certain Ben meant no disrespect whatsoever. I don't know exactly what was said, and I don't care. All I do know is that the Welsh press and public took it 100 times more to heart than I did. For weeks afterwards, I was getting questions from Welsh journalists, who were looking for a good old-fashioned row, along the lines of 'How much did Ben Cohen's remarks bother you?'

I was even having fans come up to me in the street and say, 'That bastard Cohen. Who the hell does he think he is?' Someone later explained to me what Ben had actually said, and it sounded genuine. But even if he had said it in a cocky way, it wouldn't have bothered me one little bit.

The worst thing about it was that when we met up later in another environment, Ben thought it necessary to seek me out and try to explain that he had meant nothing by it. I told him not to ever give it another thought, and I was appalled when he came to Wales a short time after with Northampton for a match against the Scarlets and was booed fervently by the crowd.

It was on to Scotland after that, but not before the outbreak of the infamous 'Grannygate' affair. Our misery after the England defeat was just the tip of the iceberg in terms of what was around the corner, with the fiasco that called into question Shane Howarth's and Brett Sinkinson's eligibility to play for Wales haunting our game for a long while after.

Grannygate didn't have much impact on me personally, over and above having to experience the rather tense atmosphere that infected the camp at the time. I was good friends with Shane, and I obviously knew Brett from Neath. It was hard to see them suffer like they did. There were a lot of things happening with it all behind the scenes, but I kept out of the politics. All I wanted to do was play and carry on getting to grips with international rugby.

I don't think it was ever either of the guys' intention to deliberately fool anybody. I just think that they got carried along by events that were out of their control, and the pity was that when it all erupted they were the ones who had to bear the brunt of it. The other lads in the team and I didn't like seeing that.

Apart from anything else, Wales lost two great players. Brett was certainly one of the best number 7s I have ever played alongside, and I've played alongside some good ones. So, from that point of view, it had a demoralising impact on the team, although I can't shed any more light on what really went on.

The Scotland game was played out against the backdrop of that storm, and we did just enough to weather it, winning 26–18. The game was a personal triumph for me, as I scored two tries, the first after I latched on to an Allan Bateman grubber kick, the second when I rounded off a good flowing second-half move. It was great to know that I could still do it at Test level after the humbling experience at Twickenham.

I think people forget that we finished the 2000 campaign with a creditable three victories out of five after we beat Ireland at Lansdowne Road in the final match, no mean achievement considering the turmoil we had been through during the previous couple of months. That win in Dublin was a nip-and-tuck affair. I remember Gareth Thomas making a try-saving tackle in the corner towards the end after Jenks had come on as a substitute and won it for us with two beautifully struck penalties. And the game was also remembered for the debut of Rhys Williams, who hadn't long broken into the Cardiff team but played like he didn't have a care in the world, making several blistering runs from deep that had Irish tacklers grabbing at thin air. It was good to see Rhys arrive, because it meant that I wasn't the only wet-behind-the-ears youngster in the side.

That game was a quieter, tougher encounter for me. I remember coming off the field at Lansdowne Road thinking that it had been another reminder, a bit like the England game had been, of how demanding international rugby could be. But I knew that no Test career was going to be plain sailing and that I had a hell of a lot to learn before I could believe that I had cracked it at the highest level.

The 2000 Six Nations had been a real learning curve for me and a good taster of what lay ahead. But those tougher times that Graham Henry had promised were only around the corner.

6

THE FALL AND THE FIGHTBACK

IF THE 2000 Six Nations had been something of a whirlwind for me, it wasn't to last. I played against Samoa that autumn in the usual November programme of matches, scoring two tries in a handsome win, and I also came on as a replacement as we pushed South Africa close in Cardiff. But after closing the book on the Six Nations in the spring of that year, I played only one more match for my country in that tournament until 2004, winning just seven caps in between, a period of almost four wasted years.

I fell out of favour with Graham Henry the season after I made my breakthrough. For reasons he is better placed to explain, he adopted a policy of big is beautiful, preferring the size of people such as Gareth Thomas and Dafydd James on the wing. While I had kept out Dafydd at times in 2000, he made a good comeback the following year when his international form won him a place on the British Lions tour to Australia and saw him impress in a series that Henry himself took charge of, one the Lions should have won instead of losing 2–1.

I did get a start against Ireland in Cardiff in October 2001 in a Six Nations match that had been postponed earlier in the year because of an outbreak of foot-and-mouth disease. There were fears that a mass migration of fans might result in the disease finding its way from the British mainland to the Emerald Isle. But maybe we'd have been better off had the fixture never been played at all, as we lost badly, 36–6, although three late tries from Denis Hickie, Brian O'Driscoll and Shane Horgan made the final scoreline look somewhat worse than our performance that day merited.

Earlier that summer, I had toured Japan with Wales while Henry was away with the Lions, an expedition that saw Lynn Howells, who was then in charge of Pontypridd, installed as head coach. It was a successful trip, in that we won both Tests in sweltering conditions: the first 53–30 and the second 64–10, a game in which I scored four tries. But, in truth, it wasn't much to write home about. With respect to Japan, they were weak, and with our best players away in Australia and the head coach not even there, I felt a bit like I was part of a sideshow.

That said, I did play well out there, with my try in the first game ranking as one of my very best solo efforts. Lynn Howells must have reported back positively about my contribution, because it won me the nod against the Irish that October. But after that game, it would be a long, long road back.

As I have already said, I didn't feel like the finished article after breaking into the Wales squad in 2000 – far from it. I knew I had much to learn. At the same time, I did not anticipate quite such a spell in the wilderness. However, 2002 and part of 2003 were periods I would rather forget about in terms of my rugby career.

As 2002 dawned, I began to fret more about my size than I had done previously. I was seeing bigger guys getting the nod for Wales and thinking that the only way I could get back in would be if I filled out, so I embarked on a campaign of doing more weights and taking more supplements, wanting the process to happen overnight so that I could make an impact as soon as possible. Everywhere I turned, the issue seemed to be about whether I was big enough for international rugby, and I started to question myself. On top of that, a lot of people I was working with in rugby were saying that they wanted me to tip the scales at a heavier weight, and it was all having an effect.

Well, I did end up putting a lot of weight on quickly, and that coupled with all the supplements I was taking was more than my body could cope with. I was walking around at a size and weight that just wasn't natural for me. The result was that I tore my hamstring five times, with both my left and right legs affected. Not only that, but I was picking up all manner of leg-muscle strains. Up to that point, I had always been the type of player who was rarely injured, and I have thankfully been the same ever since. But in 2002 I just couldn't get fit, full stop.

Worse, I felt sluggish on the field and nowhere near as sharp as I always had done. My stamina and aerobic fitness were not what they should have been because of my preoccupation with weights. I was finding that I was blowing hard towards the end of games, which was so unlike me.

Injury had kept me out of the first Six Nations game of 2002, but when we were hammered by 50 points at Lansdowne Road in the opening game, Graham Henry and the Welsh Rugby Union (WRU) parted company, and Steve Hansen took over. Because of the way I was at the time, I was dropped like a stone from the Welsh set-up. It seemed as though Steve had come in with a clean slate and had decided which players he liked and which ones he didn't. I fell into the latter category, and I began to wonder if I had played my last game for my country.

Don't get me wrong, there were plenty of times when injury

meant I wasn't available anyway. But when I was back playing, I found that I was still ignored. I used to get terribly frustrated. I felt I was good enough and should have been getting selected, but in hindsight the opposite was true. I was in no fit state to be playing for Wales. Physically, I was way off where I needed to be. Injuries had taken over my life, to the extent that every time I made a comeback for Neath my form was poor.

I also had to deal with another major setback. I previously alluded to an elbow injury that had required a skin graft after I crashed my bike. That injury has led to problems later in my career and was the reason why I needed an operation on the joint before the 2007 World Cup.

The accident was down to my own carelessness. I used to do a lot of cycling when I was a kid and had decided to take it up again at that time. I bought a new bike, but the very next day I got too confident on one of the tracks near my home, tried to take a jump too fast, and ended up coming off and knocking myself out. I had a nasty cut on my elbow, which I had smashed against the bike on impact, and needed 20 stitches. But that was just the start of my problems, because I developed septicaemia as a result of the wound and ended up spending a fortnight in hospital on a drip.

There was no sign of blood poisoning when I first went in to get the cut seen to, but when I went back the next day my arm had ballooned to twice the size that it should have been and the skin had gone purple. The doctors were alarmed and didn't mess about. They rushed me straight to hospital in Carmarthen and placed me in a room on my own. I ended up having five skin grafts and lost an entire week of my life, because I was so ill and out of it that I didn't have a clue what was going on around me.

The whole incident was kept out of the papers at the time

because I shouldn't really have been out biking, as I was recovering from a hamstring strain. After I came through, one of the doctors told me I was lucky – that had I not been fit and young, I could well have died. The injury has caused me problems later in life because I actually had a lot of the infected tissue around the elbow removed altogether. Afterwards, I could hardly move my right arm. It was so weak and prevented me from doing a lot of training.

It was after this episode that my injuries really began to affect me mentally. I look at some of the boys now who have serious injuries and wonder how they pull through. Dai Bishop at the Ospreys is one example: he had more than two years out of the game with his knees, and my Wales teammate Mark Jones went through the same thing. The way both of them came back was amazing.

When you depend on your body for your living and all of a sudden you can't trust it, it is very difficult to deal with. You begin to question why things are not working and why such and such a problem is taking so long to heal. And when you break down with the same ailment a few weeks later, you can't find any reason in your mind for it. That was what I was going through. I just wanted answers and a path to avoid the same things happening again. But it seemed as if there were never going to be any answers. I was tying myself up in all sorts of mental knots.

There were times in 2002 when I would tell my mother that I was going to give up rugby altogether. That was how down I was – I had had a gutful. I had been dropped by Wales, I couldn't train or play and my confidence was shot to bits.

To be fair, Steve Hansen did speak to me and told me not to lose heart. Before he left, Graham Henry had said that he felt I was losing a bit of confidence, but by the time Steve was in charge my negativity was starting to snowball. It got to the point that I barely wanted the ball on the field and didn't believe in my talent any more. It reached a stage that I wasn't keen on getting out of bed at all. The main reason was that I had rehab in front of me most days, and I had lost my faith in the process. It had got me nowhere previously and had only led to more injuries. If I was going to just break down again in a few weeks, what was the point of putting myself through all the effort in the first place?

By that stage, I was sinking towards depression, and I soon got myself into the dangerous habit of going out too often in the evenings and drinking, whether it was at the weekend or midweek. When I look back, it wasn't out of a need to consume alcohol and more to do with sheer boredom. I wasn't playing or training, so going out was one of the few things I could do.

I was single at the time and living on my own. That meant in my inactive state I was climbing the walls in frustration, desperate to get out of the house and do something. To put it simply, I just couldn't cope. Nothing was going right for me, and I felt like life was conspiring against me. I was inches away from hanging up my boots altogether, and if I had done that, I would probably be about 30 stone by now.

I look back on that time and am glad that I pulled through. I was so low, but it could have been a lot worse, and getting through something like that has made me a stronger character. You have to go there to come back.

When I recall that period, I sometimes criticise myself for going over the top, because the rest of my health was OK and I had no other emotional problems. But, at the end of the day, it was how I felt at the time. I was on the floor.

At the start of the 2002–03 season, I sat myself down and had a long think about the future. There were two options: I could just give up, not worry about the rehab and turn into a slob who wasted his talent, or I could train hard, get the injuries out of the way once and for all, and start playing regularly for Neath again. Thankfully, I chose the second option, but this time I had learned from my past. I still did the weights, but something clicked, and I told myself to stop obsessing about my size. I cut out the supplements I was taking and decided to concentrate on getting sharp again. I did loads of sprint training with an old fellow called Royce Grint, a crazy bloke who used to work with us at the club as a specialist pace coach. Slowly, things began to turn around for me.

I did a lot of work with Steve Richards on other aspects of my fitness and basically gave myself a kick up the backside. I had the pre-season to get myself better, and my attitude was to see how it went, to take one day at a time. If I had ended up back on the treadmill of injuries, I wouldn't be where I am now, simple as that. But it didn't turn out like that, thank God.

The pre-season went brilliantly. Not only did I do work at Neath, I also did some sessions with Amman United off my own bat, which improved my confidence even more. My attitude was the best it had ever been, and by the time the season started I was firing once more.

It was a different sort of season altogether. I told myself to start enjoying the game again, and I wasn't working myself up about playing for Wales. I just thought about international rugby as a nice little bonus that might happen again some time in the future.

We had a decent season. Bridgend won the Welsh Premiership in what was to be the final season before regional rugby came in, but the most memorable part of the year was our Heineken Cup campaign. We didn't set the world on fire, and we didn't qualify from our pool, but the experience of playing matches against Leicester and Béziers was invaluable.

The Leicester match at the Gnoll, the first of the pool, was a special night. It was windy and rainy, and the Gnoll was crammed full with about 7,000 home and away supporters. The Tigers were in their pomp at the time. They were the holders of the Heineken Cup, and the likes of Martin Johnson, Neil Back and Austin Healey still ruled the roost. It could not have been a tougher assignment for us, and it was company we weren't used to keeping, but we got a 16–16 draw out of it, which was no more than we deserved after leading for most of the night. In fact, we were 13–6 to the good at half-time after a try by our Tongan centre Dave Tiueti. But Leicester hammered away at us in the second half, and when Healey wriggled through for a brilliant individual try, it looked like curtains for us with only two minutes left of normal time. But almost immediately from the restart, their prop Franck Tournaire was penalised, and Lee Jarvis banged over a nerveless penalty to level the scores and send the Neath fans home happy.

However, the difference between the two sides was obvious in the return game at Welford Road. It spoke volumes about where we were in comparison to the best in Europe that we were able to raise ourselves for a one-off heroic effort on our own patch but were totally outclassed on enemy territory. Yet I enjoyed the experience of playing at a venue like Welford Road. We were bullied out of it up front, with Johnson in complete command, but I got a consolation try, and it felt good to be playing in that kind of high-profile affair again. By then it was January 2003, and I hoped I'd sent a little reminder to Steve Hansen.

I liked Steve. I liked his directness and the fact that he wasn't afraid to speak his mind. He was a man's man. He would tell you things straight to your face, but he was also prepared to be criticised himself if it was justified. Steve never wasted words and didn't give a toss what people thought if he believed he was right. I hated him when he wasn't picking me, but I now know that he is one hell of a coach.

I was fonder of Graham Henry than Steve, because he was the one who had brought me into the Wales family in the first place. He had nurtured me. I was really sorry to see him go. Steve came in and bluntly told me that I wasn't fit enough for his team and that he wouldn't be picking me, although he did encourage me to fight for my place and to prove him wrong. But that's little consolation as a player when you're left out. At one stage, I believed that Steve would never rate me so decided that I wasn't going to rate him. I took his rejection personally for a time, and when I look back, I realise that was a childish way to behave.

However, it seemed that I wasn't on his radar that January – for the time being. Instead, it was August of 2003 before I got a call from anyone in the Wales management team, and it almost felt like a lifetime since I had last been involved.

Wales had been whitewashed in the Six Nations of 2003, when they had lost to Italy for the first time in the opening game, and I'd probably watched all the matches in the pub. Some people were telling me that I was better off out of it, that they were a shambles and that Hansen didn't have a clue. I could understand their frustration, but if I had been called up, I wouldn't have hesitated.

There was also talk at around that time that I should be given another chance. My confidence was back, and I had put a good spell of form together for Neath. Even though there was little spectacular about the way I was playing, I felt a more complete package, and I knew for a fact that I was faster than ever, because my sprint times were down there in black and white. But I wasn't going to let myself agonise about Wales again.

By the summer, the World Cup in Australia was well and truly on the horizon, and I had done my pre-season work with the newly formed Neath–Swansea Ospreys (we are now just Ospreys), more or less believing that I wasn't going to be involved in the biggest tournament of them all. It hadn't weighed on my mind, but I would be lying if I said that I wasn't envious of those who were obviously going to be selected.

When it came, the call didn't excite me too much. It was the offer of a run-out in the final warm-up match against Romania at Wrexham, and it felt as though Hansen was just picking me so he could say that he had given me my opportunity. Deep down, I didn't think that it was a good enough chance to impress sufficiently to get on the plane to Australia, but I didn't mind that. I just tried to be positive. At least I was back in the red jersey, and if I felt that it was a fairly meaningless cap against poor opposition, then there were plenty of others in the team that night who probably felt the same way.

The game went well for me. I got a couple of tries in a predictably easy win and did some good things, but I still expected to be back training with the Ospreys a week later. But a letter arrived soon after, asking me to go to the Vale of Glamorgan Hotel to see Steve Hansen. When I got there, he told me that he already had his combinations in the back line worked out, and I began to think that I had been summoned just to be let down gently and to be given some encouragement about the future. It was then that he hit me with what was a bit of a bombshell: 'Would you mind going to the World Cup as our third-choice scrum-half?'

My first thought was, 'You cheeky bastard.' But unlike Steve, I chose not to speak my mind. Instead – and I was speaking from the heart – I said that I just wanted to go to the World Cup and would be glad of any opportunity. And so that was that. I had made the World Cup squad.

I had mixed feelings, though. I was chuffed to be going, but part of me was determined to prove a point to Steve, and another part of me didn't for a minute expect to play scrum-half at the World Cup anyway. It felt like I'd at least been given half a chance.

There was almost a bit of a tongue-in-cheek feel about the selection announcement when Steve confirmed to the media that I was indeed going as his third-choice number 9. But it turned out to be a once-in-a-lifetime experience for me, the tournament that relaunched my career. If I had felt like I was on the way to being my old self during the previous season, the World Cup of 2003 ended up catapulting me to a different level.

When we first arrived in Australia, I felt like the baggage man. I really had no expectation of figuring in any of the games. We stayed first of all in a nice big hotel on Manley beach just outside Sydney, and I rubbed my hands and thought I could handle six weeks of this sort of thing, especially given that we would get the chance to do a bit of surfing and scuba-diving. But things changed when we moved to Canberra, the Australian capital. I'm sure Canberra has a lot going for it and is great in its own way, but anyone who has been there will tell you that it is not the most exciting capital city in the world. It's a civic centre before anything else, and there's very little life there.

When we got there, we discovered that we were staying in little apartments in which we were expected to cook our own food and do our own laundry. I was paired with Robin McBryde, and I remember wondering how on earth we were going to cope. I think we ended up going out to eat most nights. The experience was brilliant, like being back at school and away on some camp. I was also fortunate that my old football pal Russell Gibbs lived in Canberra, and I spent quite a bit of time with him.

Training was difficult. Because I was on the fringe of the squad, I was always expected to be the 'opposition'. I've never been so many different countries in my life: Tonga, Italy, Canada. I didn't mind most of the time, but there were instances when it started to get on my nerves. I was the only player not to get any game time at all in the pool stages. I didn't make the squad for the matches against Canada and Italy, and although I was on the bench for the Tonga game I didn't get on. I'd defy any player not to become frustrated in those circumstances. But I didn't want to lose my head. I spoke to Steve a couple of times, and he told me I would get my chance.

However, I did flip during one training session, and the end result was a showdown with Steve afterwards. I can't recall which game we were leading up to, but it was one of the pool matches, and Steve had instructed the opposition players to kick the ball back to the team he had selected, because that is what he expected the real opponents to do in the match. Someone box-kicked the ball right into my hands, and as I caught it there was a player bearing right down on top of me, so I stepped out of his way and ran a short distance. Steve lost his head. 'Shane, I thought I told you to fucking kick the thing,' he roared.

That was it. I snapped, too: 'How am I supposed to kick it when there's a guy right on top of me? Fuck off!'

It was one of those situations when you instantly regret saying something. 'Oh my God,' I thought to myself. 'I've just told Steve to fuck off in front of everyone.'

Steve let it go at first, but he pulled me up after the session. 'I understand you're frustrated,' he said, 'but don't ever tell me to fuck off in front of my players again. I respect you standing up to me, but don't try and make me look like an idiot in front of my team.'

I told him that I felt like a bit of a joke carrying water bottles and pads about all the time. But he didn't care. He just wanted to put my attitude right, and it did stink at times. Looking back, it was good for me. I shouldn't have sworn at him like that, and I have never done so to any other coach. It was a heat of the moment thing. But I'll say one thing for Steve: he wasn't the kind to bear a grudge, as the future was to bear out. We always got on well after that.

Typically, my chance came at what I thought was the worst possible time. All week before the final pool game against New Zealand, I had been in bed with a stomach upset, but Steve came and told me that he wanted me to face the All Blacks. What great preparation to take on arguably the best team in the world: I'd been in bed for four days, I'd had to be quarantined from the rest of the squad, I hadn't trained at all and I didn't know any of the moves or calls.

It was only the day before the game that I felt better. I got up that morning and tried to get as much food down me as possible. The kick-off wasn't until the evening of the next day, and I have to admit that by then I was bouncing. All the sitting about was finally over and weeks of frustration was ready to pour out of me. I just wanted to get out there, get the ball in my hands and play. And the whole approach to the match against New Zealand suited me. As players, our mindset now that we had qualified for the quarter-finals was to go out there and give it a real good go. Steve told us the same thing. He told us that we had a stage against the best team in the world and to go out there and make the most of it.

We didn't know what to expect, and we knew we could get a 50-point hiding. But when New Zealand scored in the first couple of minutes, we got together behind the uprights and spoke about how none of us wanted to spend the evening watching

Kiwi conversions sailing through our sticks. Then things changed. It wasn't just a case of a care-free 'chuckabout'. We went through our patterns brilliantly. The type of rugby we played doesn't just materialise, it comes about as a result of months of hard work, and while I hadn't been involved in the squad until late on, I knew how strong the team's work ethic was.

We kept the ball very well and ended up playing a full part in one of the best games the World Cup has ever seen. I had a great match, but I was by no means the only one: Jonathan Thomas was sensational, too; Gareth Thomas did so well at full-back as a fourth-minute replacement for Garan Evans that he ended up playing there for years afterwards; and Ceri Sweeney also came off the bench that night to produce a superb performance.

It was one of those games in which I thought, 'Sod the game plan, just give me the ball.' I wanted to show Steve that I should have played more in the tournament, and I wasn't at all scared or worried going into it. I didn't care who I was playing against on the wing. The truth was that I didn't expect to be playing the next week anyway, so I just went out and did my thing. I played at number 9, 10, 14 and 15. I ran my heart out and never got tired.

I was so excited to be there and more aware of things around me than I had ever been. I was spotting their props out of position and targeting a run at them, the pitch seemed enormous, like there was 15 yards extra space on either flank, and everything I got involved with seemed to go well. As the game wore on, I felt as though I was getting stronger rather than tiring. I didn't want it to end, and when the final whistle did blow, I remember wishing that there had been another 15 minutes more to play.

It's easy to forget that we lost 53–37 that night, but for Wales it wasn't about the result: it was about showing the rugby world that we were back after a couple of years in the doldrums; it was about winning back our self-respect and proving that we could still play the bloody game.

When I walked off the field, I felt that I had proved my point – proved to people that I still belonged at this level. Steve said afterwards in the dressing-room that he had deliberately held me back for the game. I think he was joking. I wasn't happy that we had lost – of course I wasn't – but for me that night was all about feeling good about myself in a Wales jersey again.

I spoke to the press afterwards and made a point of saying that I hoped all those who had doubted me were now thinking differently. The game had turned my whole career around. The difference after that was huge. All of a sudden, everyone was talking about me. I now felt that there was no way Steve could drop me for the quarter-final against England. I thought that if I was dropped, it was more likely to be Steve who would cop the flak. But by that time I was determined to go with whatever decision Steve arrived at. To a certain extent, I had resented my treatment at first, but I had proved my point, and nothing could alter that.

However, I did get the nod, although it was to be the team's last hurrah in the competition. England were in town on the glory trail and were admittedly formidable, but we went into the game with a new sense of self-belief. We were by far the better side in the first half and went off leading 10–3. It would have been 14–3 had we converted our two tries. England were stunned, and we really believed we could push on and cause what would have been the upset of the decade.

After half-time, they changed tactics and wore us down up front, kicking their penalties, with Mike Catt's intelligent punting winning them good territory. I thought we should have won, but again I took a hell of a lot from the experience. The

Suncorp Stadium in Brisbane was awesome. We had lost, but we were going home on a high, and deservedly so.

When we arrived at the Vale of Glamorgan, hundreds of people were there to cheer us. It was strange because we had lost, but for me it was a happy homecoming. People didn't need to tell me I had played well. I knew in myself, and that was more important, especially as only a short time before I had been considering quitting the game altogether. I'd turned the corner, but even more unimaginable highs lay in store.

7

MY RUDDOCK VERDICT

SO MUCH has already been said and written about Mike Ruddock's memorable time as Wales coach. There have been a lot of opinions expressed and theories put forward as to what led to his controversial departure in the early months of 2006, and it is still the first question I get asked by supporters whenever I go anywhere to take part in forums. A lot of people think they know what happened, even though they weren't the slightest bit involved, and while it is one of those events that we will perhaps never totally get to the bottom of, there is also an awful lot of rubbish spouted about what happened.

Mike took over in the spring of 2004 amid a lot of hoo-ha that the WRU had supposedly done the dirty on Gareth Jenkins, who was believed to be the front runner. As players, we weren't bothered about any of that, though, and when Mike came in, he did not set about changing much from what Steve Hansen had put in place. He was of the opinion that much of what had been done previously did not need to be discarded, so many of the patterns and game plans stayed the same. It was as if Mike did not want to fix what wasn't broken, but suggestions that he just wanted to ride on the wave of what Steve had done and do as little as possible himself were unfair. Mike did have a lot of his own ideas, too, and in different circumstances could have implemented them if he had felt that they were for the best.

There were rumours that he didn't spend enough time on the training field and didn't take enough responsibility. Again, I wouldn't subscribe to that point of view. He wasn't as hands-on as Steve had been, but he worked in a different way.

There has been much criticism of Mike, but I thought he did a good job, and he was certainly good for my rugby development. I had a very good professional relationship with him. I always felt he wanted me to do well, and he always encouraged me to get as involved as possible and to keep my work rate high. He wanted the ball in my hands and for me to enjoy myself, because he knew that was when I was at my most dangerous. There was never a problem between us, and I was delighted when he agreed to coach the overseas team in my testimonial match last summer. That certainly wouldn't have happened if there had been the slightest bit of bad blood between us.

Mike has taken a lot of flak since leaving the Wales job, and for me most of it has been undeserved. A lot of people have come out and said that our training sessions were always run by players or other coaches, but I didn't see it that way. I felt his input was always as it should have been.

At the time, with the senior players we had, there were occasions in training sessions when questions were asked by the likes of Colin Charvis or Gareth Thomas about the way we were playing. But it was always open and above board, and in my opinion that is the way it should be. Senior players have to have their views taken into account, and most coaches value the feedback. However, a lot of people took it the wrong way, and rumours began that we weren't playing for Mike, that we were doing what we wanted to do on the field and that our Grand Slam success was nothing to do with him. That was just untrue.

You wouldn't be able to do that at international level and be successful. You have to have someone there guiding you.

I thought the coaching team functioned well. Mike worked well with Clive Griffiths, who was in charge of the defence, and then there was Scott Johnson, of course, a total one-off and one of the most technically gifted coaches I have ever worked with. It didn't matter who you were, what your ability was or how many caps you had, Scott would look at you as a player, spot your weaknesses and get you to work on them. He had me working on my passing, holding my depth in attack, angles of running, support play, absolutely everything that I had always assumed I did OK. He told me that I was rubbish at them all. 'Rubbish, mate,' he would bark in that Aussie drawl of his, and it was a real eye-opener for me about just how far I could still go to improve.

I did a lot of work with Scott, a lot of players did, and much of it was back to basics. He took us back to our roots. Some of the stuff he did with us was stuff I had done as an 11 year old, but it was all necessary, because I wasn't good enough at those things. Until he told me so, I hadn't realised that I was lacking in certain areas, and there is no doubt in my mind that he made me a much better player. My game came on leaps and bounds under him, and I was gutted to see him go – talk about a guy who knows his stuff.

Then there was Andrew Hore. He arrived in 2002 and was given the brief of making Wales a fit side. He did, and how. Horey constructed his own training sessions and did away with such things as long runs, bringing in shorter, sharper methods that were all enjoyable and always rugby related. He very much had a unique way of working and was enormously respected by everyone. Horey was a hard taskmaster, but if he could see that you were putting the work in, he was fine. He is small in stature, but he was not afraid to shout orders at the biggest forwards in the side and could be a nasty piece of work when he wanted to be, especially if he didn't think that you were working hard enough. I was chuffed to bits when the Ospreys got him to join us in 2007, and he has had a huge impact on every aspect of the club since he arrived. Horey is a guy who has no end of ideas but is also always open to input.

And that was very much the culture in the Wales set-up at the time. Mike took on board the views of the players, mine included, and that was healthy. There were strong characters in the squad, but the 'player power' catchphrase used by the media was blown way out of proportion.

It was a funny old time. I was stunned when Mike left the job. I hadn't a clue where his decision had come from and could never have imagined the furore it would cause in its aftermath.

We were training in the barn at the Vale of Glamorgan Hotel one afternoon when we first heard that something serious was afoot. There were rumours going around that a press conference had been scheduled for later in the day, and then one of the media people from the WRU turned up and said that Mike had gone.

'Where's he gone?' we asked.

'No, gone, as in gone altogether,' came the reply.

We were gobsmacked. One minute we were training as normal, the next we were coming to terms with a piece of news like that. Immediately, I had people calling me. 'What's this about? Why has he gone? Why are the media talking about player power?' were the kind of questions I was being asked. But I had no answers for any of them. All I could think of was that I had to try to find out what had indeed happened.

Nobody could really shed any light, though. That Sunday, Alfie (Gareth Thomas) went on *Scrum V*, the weekly rugby show on BBC Wales, to represent the players' views. I was at home watching with a few friends, and I had mixed emotions about him going on in the first place. I admired his guts for doing it, but I feared he might get outnumbered and ripped to shreds by Eddie Butler and company, who were nobody's fools. At times, the BBC lot really tried to stick the knife in, and I thought Alfie did well under the circumstances. At one stage, I thought he was going to get up and chin Butler, and I was thinking to myself, 'Don't do it, don't do it.' I was on the verge of hiding behind my settee.

In hindsight, I don't think he should have gone on the programme at all, but I know that it was Alfie who made the decision. He thought that the players were being attacked from all angles and unfairly blamed for Mike's exit, and he wanted to stand out in front of us all and defend us. We admired him for that, but, in truth, he only ended up making himself look like a scapegoat, which was unfair.

Alfie was always a players' captain first and foremost. He put the needs of his players before anything else in the world and would shield them to his dying breath. As our captain at the time, he was a real warrior, and he took the attacks on us personally. I suppose the one consolation was that the whole thing made for great TV.

Alfie had his funny turn back at his house that night, a damaged neck artery finally catching up with him and resulting in a mini-stroke that put him out for the rest of the season, but thankfully it did no lasting damage. That incident put a turbulent time into perspective. Given everything that went on in the run up to it, I wouldn't be surprised if stress was a factor.

Mike's resignation was the culmination of a sequence of events during the 2006 Six Nations that led to the virtual implosion of the team – at least temporarily – after all we had achieved in 2005. Gavin Henson's book, published after the 2005 Grand Slam, came back to haunt us as we kicked off the tournament at Twickenham. Rewind six months or so, and Gav had caused a right old stir with some of the stuff he had written in his book, which he had produced in collaboration with Graham Thomas, a journalist with BBC Wales. There was a lot of personal stuff about the boys in there, stuff about drinking habits, girlfriends and what the players were like when they were drunk. A lot of it really should have been kept private if Gav was going to continue playing alongside those guys. It would have been fine if he had been retiring or emigrating to Australia, but not when he still had the best part of a decade of his career to get through.

I was lucky, as there was nothing too revealing or derogatory about me. I wasn't surprised by that, because we have always got on well, and there is a mutual respect between us. 'Thank God you didn't write anything bad about me,' I said to him when the fuss was happening. He laughed, and I thought to myself that he probably would have done if he had remembered anything.

But some of what he wrote struck a real nerve with some of the others. I wasn't offended personally, but I could totally understand why some of them were. I actually found it quite funny, because I have a fair idea of how it happened, knowing Gav as I do. He is a bloke who speaks his mind without really giving any thought to the consequences. He's always been the same, even in newspaper interviews. He's a bit of a journalist's dream, to be honest.

What I find hard to understand is why those who were advising him didn't foresee the furore that his book was likely to cause. I really don't think that Gav meant any harm, but what happened during the aftermath was incredible. His book was serialised by the *Western Mail*, and once a few headlines were placed next to his opinions, the whole thing blew up everywhere, like nothing else in the world mattered. Once the newspaper got hold of it, the impact it had in Wales was amazing.

The funniest part of it all for me was when Gav was called in to face the players about it. The meeting was designed to clear the air once and for all, because there were some reports in the media that he would never be welcome in the Wales squad again. We arranged the chairs in a half-circle and put one solitary chair facing us all for him to sit in. Gav strolled in without a care in the world. 'What's up boys?' he said, as if he couldn't for the life of him understand why there was a problem. That was enough for some of the lads.

'What's up? What's up?' someone said furiously. 'Do you know why you're here?'

'Oh, it's about the book, is it?' said Gav, still cool as a cucumber.

I was squirming at the back, praying that he would quickly say sorry and have done with it. I wanted to laugh, but I couldn't because I knew that some of the boys were truly offended. Colin Charvis was fuming, and Gethin Jenkins wanted to throttle him, but Gav being Gav just listened to each gripe and said things like, 'Oh yeah, sorry about that one . . .'

'But it's too late for that. It's in the book now.'

'What if we did a book and put stuff about you in it?' one of the boys said.

Gav just looked at him as if butter wouldn't melt and said, 'Go for it, butt. No worries.' There wasn't really any answer to that. And I know that if ever something negative actually was written about Gav in someone's book, he wouldn't care two hoots.

The meeting wasn't exactly ideal, but in its own way it did clear the air. Gradually, the whole episode was pushed into the background, and Gav was integrated back into the squad. I wouldn't mind betting that there was a grudging admiration among some of the lads for the fact that he was willing to face us all like that in the first place.

Anyway, by the time we got around to playing England in February 2006, the first match of that year's Six Nations, we thought that the whole thing had been put behind us, but it was dredged back up by Graham Thomas in an article in the match-day programme that really annoyed some of the lads. The result was the boycotting of a press conference before the Scotland game when the BBC reporter turned up, having been asked not to do so by the team management. We all felt strongly about it, and Mike ended up having to face the media on his own, which just led to more conjecture about what was going on behind the scenes. How much that little episode contributed to his departure, I don't know, but it didn't exactly help.

Mike's first assignment when he took charge was a tour of Argentina, with a two-Test series planned in one of the harshest rugby environments there is. And it was a mixed start for the new coach. We lost the first Test against the Pumas 50–44 in Tucumán, a scoreline that was more akin to a Barbarians match. There were a staggering eleven tries in all – we got five of them – but both defences were like sieves, and as a team we were all at sea, at one stage trailing 38–9. But we bounced back in Buenos Aires a week later to win 35–20, ironically against a stronger Argentina outfit than we had faced a week before. After a week of hard work trying to rectify the mistakes of the first match, we produced a much tighter display and never looked back from a blistering first-half show in which I scored three tries to help craft a 25–0 lead. The second of those scores was one of my very best. I ran in from deep, carving my way through a series of Puma defenders. Although they threw the kitchen sink at us in the first period of the second half, we were convincing winners by the end. We were tired as we headed home and lost 53–18 to South Africa in Pretoria on the way back, but despite the margin of that defeat, it wasn't too bad a start for Mike, all things considered.

We continued to improve in the autumn internationals that year, pushing New Zealand to within a point in Cardiff, losing 24–23, and also running the Springboks to within two points. I felt Mike was having a good effect on us. I thought the forwards in particular were benefiting from what he was bringing to the table, and as a unit we were in very good stead for the 2005 Six Nations.

We didn't expect to win the Grand Slam, but the autumn internationals had shown us that we were capable of winning against the big sides, and we went into the tournament with far more self-belief than usual. We got the win against England, with me scoring the only try in an 11–9 victory and Gavin Henson scoring the last-minute penalty that proved to be the springboard we needed. Looking back, it was like we were meant to win that game, that it was written in the stars, and doing so gave us a massive boost of confidence.

We followed that up with what everyone thought would be a difficult trip to Italy in the second round of matches. But it just showed what frame of mind we were in, as we hammered them 38–8 at the Stadio Flaminio. I scored what I consider to be one of my best-ever tries, rounding off a flowing move that began when Alfie made a break up the middle of the pitch. Everything went right for us that day, our patterns were spot-on and some of our attacking play was simply devastating. I don't think the Italians knew what had hit them, to be honest – we were that good.

Things snowballed from there, and the next win, against France in Paris, was just sensational, with many people since saying to me that it is one of the best Wales victories they have ever witnessed. I was marking their big winger Aurélien Rougerie, and he ran over me a couple of times in the early exchanges when we were massively under the cosh. I'll admit that I feared the worst at that stage, but amazingly we managed to get in at half-time only trailing 15–6 and still very much in it.

Again, it felt almost as if we were meant to win that game. Martyn Williams got those two quick tries early in the second half, and the defensive effort in the closing stages of the game was just monumental. I was off the field at that point and was just praying we would keep them out. If you look at the TV footage of the match, it looks for all the world as if the French are going to score, but every time one of our boys was required to make a tackle, it was made. The relief I felt when Stephen Jones booted the ball over the dead-ball line to signal the end was something I will never forget.

The match against Scotland at Murrayfield was different from the others that year, especially the one in France. Traditionally, Edinburgh has been a difficult place for us to go to, but we brushed the Scots aside. Again, some of the rugby we played in the first half was breathtaking. We were throwing the ball around like it was an exhibition game at times. I think, had we not taken our collective foot off the gas in the final quarter, we could have completely humiliated the Scots in front of their own fans with a points tally into the 60s. But it hardly mattered. We were playing Ireland in Cardiff for the Grand Slam – and what a day that proved to be.

Everything about it was perfect. The sun shone, and we produced a display against a strong Irish outfit that meant we were always in charge from the moment Gethin Jenkins charged down a punt from Ronan O'Gara to run through and score. That incident was the end of O'Gara that day. His head dropped, and he wasn't anywhere near as influential as we knew he could be.

In every department, we swarmed around them and stifled their threat. I thought that Tom Shanklin did a real number on O'Driscoll in the midfield, and Gav was on fire again. Martyn Williams had yet another great game, and we were deserving winners by the time the final whistle sounded.

We had a brilliant do that night at the pub in Brains Brewery in the centre of Cardiff. Unfortunately, I drank too much and was carried back to my hotel room by John Williams, the Welsh team doctor, missing out on the chance to continue the celebrations with the rest of the boys in the pubs and clubs of the city. I woke up the next morning, still fully clothed, and immediately wondered how I was going to get through another day's drinking that had been planned by the boys. Then, to add insult to injury, my phone bleeped with a text message telling me that I had half an hour before I had to speak to the press.

I slumped back on the bed, knowing that I was in serious trouble because of my hangover. I was excused the formal press conference, but I did do a couple of TV interviews, and I must have looked like death warmed up.

Somehow we headed out to restart the party that Sunday afternoon, or 'Super Sunday' as we called it. I started to feel better fairly quickly, and it was a good job because it was carnage in The Yard, the pub in Cardiff where we celebrated. I didn't get into a state again. I was more sensible, or as sensible as I could be, and really enjoyed myself. We went around a few pubs and had a great reception from people wherever we went.

I got up the next morning feeling fine and headed home – where the revelry began again, this time with my family and friends. Those few days were the best demonstration of how much the success of the rugby team means to people in Wales.

When we do well, you feel that the whole country has been lifted.

That week was a blur, and I was on cloud nine. They were such good times. But, for me, what happened to Mike in the aftermath put a dampener on the whole achievement. I suppose that's what happens in Welsh rugby, though.

After he had gone, Scott Johnson took temporary charge of the team, but the 2006 Six Nations just petered out for us in what was a huge comedown from 2005. There was so much negative publicity flying around, and I could see that it took its toll on the players, no matter what was said to the contrary. We felt as though we were back to square one. We had a lot of injuries, but we should still have had the strength in depth to do better.

I missed the games against Ireland and Italy that followed Mike's exit. The match in Dublin was awful. I watched it on television, and everyone looked so uncomfortable, with Gavin especially out of sorts after coming on as an early substitute at fly-half when Stephen Jones picked up a dead leg.

It was typical of Welsh rugby down the years. One minute we were in the middle of a national celebration, the next we were ripping each other apart amid a string of defeats and inquests into what had gone wrong and who was to blame.

I was glad to see the back of the 2006 campaign, but I knew we had not seen the last of Mike Ruddock in rugby, and sure enough he has come back strong at Worcester, where he appeared to be really making his presence felt in the second half of last season as the club's results steadily improved after a shaky start in the Guinness Premiership. There was also an appearance in the European Challenge Cup final.

Mike had a little spell out of the game altogether, and I didn't blame him for wanting time away, but I knew he would be back

– and back successfully. The signings he made at Worcester, including Ricoh Gear and Chris Latham, demonstrated Mike's ambition, and I think they will enjoy working with him. The thing I like about Mike is that he is very down to earth and always approachable, but he hates losing. When he has a task in front of him, he wants to do it well, and he loves a challenge, which he certainly has at Worcester.

I don't think it's any coincidence that almost every high-profile player who has worked under Mike has nothing but good things to say about the way he works, and you certainly won't find me bad-mouthing him. To be honest, it's not my style. I'm the sort of person who is always very respectful of coaches, and I genuinely have never worked underneath a coach at professional level who I thought didn't know what he was doing.

Let's get one thing straight, coaching a professional rugby team is a bloody hard job. There are so many things you have to get right to be successful, so if someone has made it to become an international coach, then they must, in my book, be doing something right – they must have something about them.

Don't get me wrong, I have disagreed with some of the things coaches have done, but on the whole I have never disrespected them – other than my heated words with Steve Hansen, of course, but that was just a one-off incident. At Test level, I've worked with Graham Henry, Steve Hansen, Scott Johnson, Mike Ruddock, Gareth Jenkins and Warren Gatland. That's not a bad collection to have learned from, and all of them, as far as I am concerned, are damn good at what they do – their track records prove as much. Yes, they have made mistakes, but not half as many as the players who have played under them.

As far as I am concerned, Mike Ruddock was instrumental in our 2005 Grand Slam, and to back that up I'll give one example of when he really earned his corn – at half-time in Paris, when we had been battered by France and looked like we were on course to go down by 50 points. It was just the way he spoke, the way he addressed us at a moment when dark clouds were hovering and our season was threatened with collapse. Mike was inspiring. Instead of ranting about our shortcomings in what had been an appalling first-half display, he told us that he thought France had thrown their best at us and that we had weathered the storm superbly.

'You've held out, but you have so much more to give,' he said. 'Let's get out there and show them what we are about. Let's perform like we know we can.' You would have had to have been in that room to understand the effect of Mike's words. He also managed to get into the heads of certain individuals. He sat down with a few players one-to-one after speaking to the whole group, and I was one of those he singled out. Mike knew that the caning I had taken from Rougerie had dented my confidence, so he made sure he sought me out. 'Don't worry about those things,' he told me. 'They have gone now. Think of the second half as your turn to give him trouble. You know you are capable of doing that.' They were exactly the words I needed to hear, and they got me thinking positively as I made my way back out onto the pitch. I am convinced that the way Mike handled himself at half-time that day had a major bearing on what subsequently happened – one of the best comebacks in Wales's history in my opinion.

Man-management was one of Mike's real strengths. He gave me a lot of time on a one-to-one basis, and I found that he had a quiet determination that seemed to rub off on me.

It was weeks before we learned anything at all about why Mike had gone. All I can say is that rather than all the conspiracy theories about player power, it was more a case of an unfortunate coming together of a lot of factors. I had a beer with him after the Ospreys played Worcester in the EDF Energy Cup last season, and it was great to catch up.

Mike has had a tough time of it in the last few years, even though he has moved on. It is clear that Alfie and Martyn – who both made their feelings known in their books – and maybe some of the other lads had issues with the way Mike ran things. As captain at the time, Alfie was a very big personality, and there were accusations that the players were playing for him more than for Mike. I never believed that for a minute, and, in my view, Alfie was unfairly vilified as a result of the whole business. I don't in any way begrudge Alfie and Martyn their opinions. They are entitled to them, and I understand where they were coming from with a lot of their views. Also, perhaps there were things going on behind the scenes that I never knew about. But I speak as I find, and my views on Mike are different.

We did sometimes have training sessions that Mike didn't attend, and there were occasions when he made changes to what the senior players were doing, but none of that was ever an issue for me. I suppose I'm just not a particularly deep thinker in those situations; I'm more like a robot. I just train and get on with it without questioning things. I was never really bothered when Mike wasn't at training, because we had other coaches, and I thought it was normal that the work be delegated to them. It never affected me, and I did my own training anyway.

I have never played any differently under any of the coaches Wales have had. I just go out and do my thing. But then my game is probably less structured than that demanded by other positions, which may be why I didn't notice the problems so much.

What can I say? I've always got on well with coaches – maybe too well with the likes of Gareth and Mike – which has perhaps prevented me from seeing the bigger picture. Am I being naive?

I don't know. I don't think so. I'm the sort of bloke who looks at the positives, and nothing will alter my opinion that Mike Ruddock did a good job. It was just a pity that he never finished it. Instead, it was Gareth Jenkins who was charged with the task of picking up the pieces.

8

THE TOUGHEST RUGBY OF MY LIFE

IT MIGHT not have been a successful tour, but my experience of being a British Lion in New Zealand was certainly one I won't forget in a hurry. They say that it is the ultimate honour in the game, and while I wouldn't place it above playing for Wales, I wouldn't disagree that there is something very special about the Lions. The feeling when I was selected was incredible. But we were taught a huge lesson by Graham Henry's All Blacks. And I can say without hesitation that it was the toughest rugby I have ever played in my life.

The main disappointment for me was that I only played in the second Test out of three. I wasn't chosen for the first Test and missed the last one through a niggling back injury. But at least I did come home with a Test appearance to my name, and I cherish that.

People say to me that I must have been confident of going on the tour beforehand, because I had just won the Grand Slam with Wales, and I had played a full part in the team's success. It stood to reason that the Wales contingent was going to be bigger than it would have been had we not had a good Six Nations. But I'm someone who never counts his chickens when it comes to selection. I had my fingers crossed, but that was about all. I knew that there are always a lot of guys who don't make it on Lions tours who you think should have done, and while the Welsh boys were on the crest of a wave, Sir Clive Woodward was an English coach and he was obviously going to have his favourites, guys he had worked with and whom he felt wouldn't let him down.

I found out that I had been selected when I was on my way home from an Ospreys match against Connacht in Galway. We were at Shannon Airport, and we had been told that if we were selected we would receive a text message. I remember looking at a television in the airport, and there was a text bar going across the screen that said the Lions squad was due to be announced shortly. I was sitting with Gavin Henson and Duncan and Adam Jones, and I can recall thinking that we would surely have known by then if we were in or not. But it was literally five minutes before they announced the squad on TV that we got those all-important texts: 'Congratulations, you have been selected for the British and Irish Lions in New Zealand. Clive.'

Obviously, there were a lot of other Wales boys in the Ospreys team, and I can remember being happy that I had received my message but also looking around with a bit of trepidation to see who else had been contacted. It was a bit of an awkward situation, because my and Gav's phones had gone off, but Adam Jones's hadn't, and after the fine Six Nations he had had, he was disappointed not to be selected. So, we tried not to make too much of a fuss about it, even though we were obviously chuffed to bits.

There were a few others who weren't picked: Ryan Jones was one – he was great for Wales that year – and Brent Cockbain another. Although both those guys came out to join the tour later when there were injuries, they were not included initially, and they were also disappointed.

After a few minutes, people came up to me and Gav to say well done, but the atmosphere was a bit strange. Deep down we were ecstatic, but we didn't want to rub anyone else's nose in it.

Not for one second did I ever imagine that I would play for the Lions, and on the flight back I thought about what it all meant. Even still, the feeling of elation didn't compare to when I was chosen by Graham Henry to play for Wales at that trial at St Helen's five years earlier.

My Lions jersey is still in the house – we don't get caps as such – and I still have lots of the kit, though I have given a lot away to charity and to my mates. My brother wears it, and I see my mates in my socks every now and then. In fact, it sometimes seems as though half of the valley is walking around in my Lions kit!

I have two jerseys, actually. Both are framed, one showing the back of the shirt with the number and the other the front. It is difficult to put all my shirts on display because I don't have the room, so most of that sort of stuff is just packed away. I have about 40 Wales shirts – I haven't framed all of them – and I suppose a lot of them will end up being given away to charity.

To say the least, the 2005 Lions party was different from previous ones. It was huge in number – players and coaches, that is – and led by a World Cup-winning coach who had a reputation for making sure players had everything they could possibly want. We were initially based in what were familiar surroundings for the Welsh boys at the Vale of Glamorgan Hotel, and that was a good start as far as I was concerned. The more little things that I felt comfortable with the better – because I was intimidated going into the Lions environment.

Yes, even though I had won a Grand Slam, been to a World Cup and played international rugby for five years, I had similar feelings to those I mentioned when I first linked up with the

Wales squad, though not nearly as bad. Back then I had been not just intimidated, but frightened. The Lions squad contained an awful lot of boys who were icons of the world game, huge names who had been around a long time, been there and done it all, and won everything there was to win. Brian O'Driscoll, Lawrence Dallaglio, Jason Robinson, Richard Hill . . . I could go on. And there were moments when I doubted whether I belonged in their company. The Lions set-up and the way Clive was doing things came naturally to those guys, but it was a different world to me, and I know some of the other Wales players found it tough to deal with at first.

Despite the sprawling size of the squad, which contained quite a few egos, we got on tremendously well together. I thought Jason Robinson and Mark Cueto, who were rivals for my position, were great guys, as was Matt Dawson. I had heard stories about Dawson and expected him to be arrogant and not have much time for someone like me, but nothing could have been further from the truth. I found him to be down to earth, friendly and easy-going.

It's vital on a Lions tours that you build relationships off the field with your teammates, because you are together for such a long time. It's different from touring with Wales, when you already know everyone and everyone knows you. With the Lions, you are pitched together with blokes you normally play against. You might have given some of them a bit of verbal during a Six Nations game, and there are inevitably a lot of preconceived ideas floating around. The challenge is to speak as you find, to discover what really makes guys from different countries tick and to get on their wavelength. Lions tours are a test of your social skills as much as anything else. There were times when we had a drink together and played a bit of golf, and, to be honest, I didn't find it difficult to form bonds with plenty of the guys.

One night in the hotel restaurant, we were split up into different teams and given the task of performing short sketches in front of the rest of the party. Some of the boys thought that it was a real laugh, others couldn't see beyond the massive embarrassment that it caused. Most of the groups acted out scenes from TV game shows. I can't for the life of me remember what game we did, but I know I played one of the contestants. Ben Kay, the English second row, was very outgoing and took to it naturally. His group played out a scene from *Bullseye*. Another bizarre sight was Gareth Jenkins playing the part of Tom Jones, who by some strange twist had become one of the other contestants. The whole thing was a bit crazy but was seen as a great way to break the ice.

As I say, some people, including Ben Kay, took it in their stride, whereas other people, such as Gavin Henson and I, were absolutely mortified. Looking back now, it was fun, but at the time the idea of making a fool of myself in front of guys whom I already found intimidating was petrifying. I'm a shy person, and I shit myself.

Our first outing on the field was against Argentina in Cardiff before we left for New Zealand. It was one of those occasions when the sheer strength of our line-up meant that most outsiders expected it to be a breeze. But it was the opposite. We had so little time in real terms to prepare for the match, and the result was a rather muddled display against a Pumas side who were determined to show us up. I didn't play that night, but we all felt the responsibility to improve after a late Jonny Wilkinson drop goal salvaged a draw and prevented us from humiliation.

Jonny has a reputation for being an obsessive trainer who has no time for anything else in his life but rugby. I suppose his dedication means that he has gone further than most others, and he did train harder than the rest of us, staying out to do two hours of kicking practice after sessions as a matter of course. But I found that there was more to him than just the game. He would chill out as well, and he wasn't 24/7 rugby. He knew how to relax. What I will say, though, is that he strikes me as a real student of the game who would think nothing of spending some of his spare time analysing things. I am entirely different. As soon as I am off the field, I like to switch off and think about something else.

We were certainly grateful that he had practised his drop goals that night, although the result, despite howls of despair from some quarters, didn't really matter compared to what we did on Kiwi soil. When we touched down in New Zealand, the real business began.

One of the first things I noticed on arrival was the sheer number of coaches that had travelled. There were big hitters, such as Andy Robinson, Eddie O'Sullivan and Gareth Jenkins, as part of the back-up staff, and there were all manner of others in different areas so that the entire Lions management group totted up to a staggering 26 people. The difficulty was that we seemed to be chopping and changing from one session to the next, with different people giving us different messages. I wasn't used to that, and I found it difficult to come to terms with.

The backs spent most of their time with Eddie O'Sullivan, Gareth Jenkins worked mainly with the forwards and there were defence sessions with Phil Ford. Clive would then maybe come and chip in for a little while at the end of the session. It did get confusing and very congested with the number of players and coaches who were around, though I wouldn't say that the training was harder than what I was used to.

Eddie O'Sullivan was very intense and worked closely with Brian O'Driscoll, not only because he was the Lions captain, but because the pair had a close relationship from working together

What an angel!
(Courtesy of the author)

Me (left), Dean and my nan.
(Courtesy of the author)

Amman Juniors. I'm in the front row, far left.
(Courtesy of the author)

My two favourite girls!
Georgie and Gail.
(Courtesy of the author)

She's getting heavier every day.
(Courtesy of the author)

Me, Mum and Dad in my early days.
(Courtesy of the author)

Yes, it is me!
(© Huw Evans Picture Agency)

Scoring for Wales against Scotland in the 2000 Six Nations.
(© Huw Evans Picture Agency)

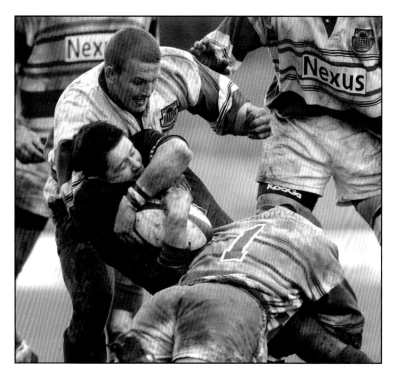

I've never been afraid to take a hit!
(© Huw Evans Picture Agency)

Not even Jonny Wilkinson could catch me at the 2003 World Cup.
(© Huw Evans Picture Agency)

Parading the 2005 Grand Slam trophy. What a day! (© Huw Evans Picture Agency)

Me, Gav, Lawrence Dallaglio and Donncha O'Callaghan at a fashion shoot before the 2005 Lions tour. (© Huw Evans Picture Agency)

Not a bad pairing. Jason Robinson supports me on Lions duty. (© Huw Evans Picture Agency)

Me and Gail on our wedding day
– 23 December 2005.
(© Huw Evans Picture Agency)

Me, Gareth Jenkins and
Martyn Williams meet
some bloke called Brown at
a Labour Party celebration
at Wembley Stadium.
(Courtesy of the author)

Get in there!
I celebrate
a crucial try
against Ireland at
Croke Park. Tom
Shanklin looks
like he approves.
(© Huw Evans
Picture Agency)

Triple Crown in the bag – and it feels good.
(© Huw Evans Picture Agency)

Touchdown! Try number 41 against France as we clinch the Grand Slam,
the score that broke Alfie's record. (© Huw Evans Picture Agency)

Lift off! I love scoring tries. This one is against Italy in our 47–8 win on the way to the 2008 Grand Slam.
(© Huw Evans Picture Agency)

I haven't always got the better of Bryan Habana.
(© Huw Evans Picture Agency)

I have always loved playing football.
(© Huw Evans Picture Agency)

for Ireland. Brian was a damn good skipper. Everyone certainly respected him, and he was influential. I liked that he led by example. He gave his all in every situation, and he expected the same of all the players. He certainly did not deserve to have his tour ended in such cruel and controversial fashion in the opening few minutes of the first Test.

So much has been said about the incident with Tana Umaga and Kevan Mealamu that saw Brian spear tackled to the floor, resulting in a broken collarbone. My view is that it was dangerous play, no question. The camera doesn't really lie on that score. But I do not for a minute buy the theory that Brian was targeted from the outset or that the two New Zealand players intended to cause such an injury. Don't get me wrong, there are instances all the time of players being singled out before matches for a bit of a roughing up, but never, in my experience, to do that kind of damage. On another day, Brian would have just landed with a bump, been treated by the physio for a few minutes and then carried on with no lasting ill-effects. That said, it was reckless play, and the boys felt desperately sorry for him. The pity for the tour was that the episode became the sole focus for the media from that time on, which ensured that the last few weeks were played out in a bitter atmosphere.

I know Gareth Thomas felt very strongly that Umaga and Mealamu were out of order, and he was right next to the incident when it happened. I wasn't selected for that first Test so didn't have such a good view. Perhaps I would have felt differently if I had.

Was I gutted to miss that game? Yes, but I was not surprised. I didn't think that I had played enough up to that point to really drive home a case for inclusion, and with such a large squad I wasn't the only one to feel like that. You get an inkling in training before matches about whether or not you are going to figure, because you find yourself watching more than being involved in the planning of moves. Everything seemed to be pointing towards the inclusion of Jason Robinson, Josh Lewsey and, of course, Alfie, who had arrived late because of commitments with Toulouse, in the back three. Therefore, when the squad for the first match was announced, it didn't come as a shock to me. And there wasn't a consoling pep talk from any of the coaches; instead, it felt to me as if their attitude was that you shouldn't have too great an expectation of being selected in the first place because there were so many players.

The problem on a Lions tour is that after the elation of being chosen to go on the trip itself, every player soon fixes their sights on playing a part in the Test matches, because they are seen as the only ones that really matter. They are the benchmark of the entire trip and the only thing that will be remembered in years to come.

History has shown us that a lot of guys just can't deal with rejection on that front – the transition from being one of the first names on the team sheet with their country to being a smaller fish in a bigger pond with the Lions. But failing to deal with it just makes the whole situation worse. My approach was not to give up, and I got something of a reward in the match against Manawatu a few days before the second Test when I ran in five tries. Granted, Manawatu were without doubt the weakest side we faced, being the only National Provincial Championship team on the schedule, and our mammoth 109–6 win told its own story. But, nevertheless, I still stood out, and I had a decent performance against Otago the previous week to add to the mix as well.

There was a general clamour for change after the 21–3 hiding the All Blacks had given us in the first Test, and a lot of people in the press were trying to advance my claim. In the end, I got the nod for the second outing in Wellington, on the left wing, and this time all the indications in the build-up had been different. I had been far more involved and had had far more dialogue with the coaches.

The outlook of the tour changed at that point, too, with Alfie taking over from Brian as captain because of his injury and injecting his unique style into the proceedings. Alfie has his own ways and methods. Both are great captains, but Alfie is just that bit more gregarious and outspoken. A lot of the guys from the other countries probably hadn't experienced leadership like it in their lives. We used to call him 'Captain Clean Off', as in clean off his head.

Alfie's personality is well known. He has a down-to-earth Bridgend brand of humour, and he refused to change it just because he was captain. In one team run before the second Test, there was a really serious atmosphere. We had just had a very poor training session, during which there had been a lot of mistakes, and Clive seemed really unhappy. We stood in a huddle, and Alfie prepared to give us a talk. 'Right, boys, we're dropping all these passes,' he said, 'but I've got two words to say to you all: don't fucking panic.' It went silent for a moment, before a grin came over his face as he realised his mistake, and everyone just exploded with laughter. After that, the whole mood changed, and we picked things up. That was the impact Alfie could have on things. He is one of the hardest workers in the game, but he knows how to combine hard work with enjoyment. That is what he brought to the Lions trip, and the boys who had not worked with him before loved him.

But not even Alfie could stem the All Black tide when it came down to it. There was the briefest moment of hope when he scored underneath the posts early on in Wellington, but that was quickly extinguished as they came back to thrash us 48–18 and take the series all too easily.

For a couple of minutes, we felt that they were beatable, but they shut that belief down ruthlessly, and as far as I am concerned that All Black side was the best there has ever been. I'm sure there will be protests about that view, but that is just my opinion. What took my breath away more than anything else was their winning attitude. There was just no way that they were ever going to lose those Test matches, and they played harder than they had probably ever played to make sure of it, harder certainly than they did in the Tri Nations or the World Cup.

We had the best players Britain and Ireland could muster, but we had no answer to what they threw at us, and that was not only a shedload of skill and physicality, but a pride I had never previously encountered. There was no way they were going to allow a British and Irish Lions team to come to their territory and win. We didn't just lose; we never got a sniff.

And I will say it again: it was the toughest rugby I have ever experienced. In the first match I played in, against New Zealand Maori, I got absolutely battered. I was hit hard when I had the ball, and I took a few digs when I didn't have it as well. The match really rattled me, and I can remember thinking afterwards, 'My God, I hope all the games aren't as physical as this.' All I can say is that when I eventually got home from the tour, my body was in bits. I had bumps and bruises all over, and I ached from head to toe.

I've played in South Africa, Argentina and Italy, places where the talk always centres on what kind of bashing you're going to take, but what singled out that New Zealand tour was the mix of physicality, high standard of play and winning attitude. In all the games we played, we were made to feel as though we were invading their manor and that they didn't want us on their turf. Even in the provincial matches, the ferocity of the tackling was a notch up from what I had seen anywhere before.

They were so proud, as if a loss to the Lions was a matter of personal honour.

We had high hopes going out there, and we knew we had great players. We had all played against New Zealand in the past and knew that they were formidable. But I don't think any of us deep down expected the black tornado that hit us.

I may face worse before I finish playing, and you should approach future matches expecting that, but the experience is also a source of reassurance, as if nothing will ever be as tough as what I faced in New Zealand. I've been hammered by Springbok tackles in Test matches, but nothing can compare to the physical and mental package that playing in New Zealand represents. An example was that even in the third Test, when they had the series in the bag, they gave every last effort that they had. It would have been easy for them to go through the motions or give a couple of per cent less. If anything, they were even more physical.

I met with Graham Henry and Steve Hansen after we lost the series in the second Test, and I could tell that they were proud of their team – rightly so – but our conversation was more of a catch up away from rugby. It was also good to mix with the New Zealand boys, who, like the Welsh, know how to let their hair down and have a drink. Richie McCaw, for example, one of the best players in the world, is one of the nicest blokes you could wish to meet, and I get on very well with him.

And I suppose it says it all that what I encountered off the field sticks in my memory as readily as some of what happened on it. The fans who had travelled out with us were just incredible – the sheer numbers blew your mind. I probably bumped into more Welsh people I knew in Wellington and Auckland than I would have done on a stroll through the Amman Valley. There seemed to be more people from Wales out there than from any of the other nations, which goes to show how much we love our rugby.

But if we love rugby, the Kiwis are totally fanatical about it. They're on another level entirely. It's a religion for them. There are six rugby channels on television, with some programmes consisting of panels of experts discussing issues affecting the game and others looking back at great All Black moments of the past – they're spoiled for choice. In Britain, there are billboards with Premier League footballers on them; in New Zealand the All Blacks are their sporting megastars, bigger than the likes of David Beckham or Cristiano Ronaldo any day of the week. It was a real eye-opener for me. When we went out for a walk and were recognised as British Lions, people would bend over backwards to do things for us. No job was too difficult.

In the days before the final Test, me and a few of the others who had been ruled out by injury – Gordon Darcy, Chris Cusiter, Gavin Henson and Gareth Cooper – went down to Queenstown on Lake Wakatipu, with Gav's mate Dai joining us for good measure. It was one of the maddest couple of days of my life. It was intended to be a break for us, and there were other players who weren't figuring in the final Test down there with their wives. The bonus was that our accommodation was all paid for by the Lions as a bit of a gift – another example of how well we were catered for.

We were determined to let off a bit of steam, but we ended up letting off a bit more than we had bargained for. We arrived in the afternoon and went straight on the beer, staying out all day and finishing off at a club that night. There was a real sense of relief that the tour was over. This was a last hurrah, and we were in good spirits despite everything that had happened over the previous six weeks or so.

After a day on the booze, we went back to the hotel, where

Gavin Henson had this idea that none of us should sleep that night. What could we do but go along with it, and every time anyone started to nod off, they were given a dig or a poke. But the problem was that his mate Dai and I had booked a bungee jump for first thing the following morning, and we were already worried enough about that without trying to do it after a sleepless night. I had agreed to do the jump after a few beers, but I was starting to have serious second thoughts. I'm terrified of heights at the best of times, and this involved jumping off one of the tallest bridges in the town and being dunked in the river below.

We turned up at the place still drunk, and, to be honest, I think that was the only reason I managed to get through it. I turned white up at the top. I felt dreadful, and the fact that Gav, Gareth and the others were laughing at me from down below hardly helped. I started to sober up with fear, and I was sweating like a pig, with visions of the cord snapping running through my mind. I turned to Dai and said that I didn't think there was any way I could go through with it, but we stayed in the queue until we heard the dreaded words, 'Right, you're next.' The bloke in charge could see how petrified I was and suggested I jump with a companion, so I grabbed hold of Dai. We strapped ourselves together. Dai was as scared as me, except not as vocal. Before we knew it, we'd been shoved off and were plummeting down head first.

It was amazing. The water was ice cold when we hit it, but the relief afterwards was incredible. It was something I was overjoyed to have done but wouldn't want to do again.

Even after that, we carried on drinking and went straight through the day again. We were in a bar by 11.30 a.m., singing karaoke, drinking lager, eating from a buffet and smoking cigars! It was like we had won the World Cup!

While we were singing away and making general fools of ourselves, a guy came up to us and asked if he could take our photographs. We asked him who he was and said that we were concerned he might hand it to the newspapers, but he assured us that he wasn't a journalist and that the picture was just for him, so we played along.

When we got back to Auckland, I received an email from Andrew Hore. It contained a picture of the back page of one of the New Zealand papers, and there we were in all our drunken glory. But by that time, we didn't care. We laughed it off and were just glad to have had such a good time. I know we didn't go to New Zealand to spend days like that, but the Queenstown experience added to the tour for me. It was a weekend that never seemed to end.

So what lessons are there to be learned from the 2005 tour to New Zealand? Well, I think that if you are going on tour with a big squad, you have to select the team you intend to play in the Test matches a lot more often during the warm-up games. The mixing and matching just didn't work for us in 2005, and having such a large group didn't pay off.

The argument to take fewer people is all well and good, but when you look at the number of injuries we had – and on Lions tours injuries are part and parcel – it's hard to justify taking a reduced party. It's more about the balance that you strike. Maybe guys should be given an indication as to whether they are more likely to play in the provincial matches before they go so it is easier to polish up a Test team in the time you have. They could still travel with the proviso that they do very much have a chance to force their way into the Test team if their form demands it or there are injuries in their position. But whether guys would want to go on that basis and whether it would be feasible, I don't know. Perhaps there is just no easy answer. You can only put 15 players onto a rugby field at a given time, but in the modern game you also need a big crop of players to call upon.

Then there is the size of the coaching pool. If I was a head coach, I don't think I would take as many support staff with me. You can argue about strength in numbers, but you also need clarity of message as well, and some of that gets lost if there are too many chiefs. I suppose the key is to find someone to lead the tour who is capable of fostering a massive sense of unity among an extended group.

Organising a Lions tour must be a thankless task. Keeping a party of more than thirty professional rugby players happy for six weeks is nigh on impossible. Some will be sacrificed for the greater good along the way, and it's minimising the negative impact of that which is key. That seems to be something Ian McGeechan managed to do in South Africa in 1997.

New Zealand 2005 was a mixed experience for me. Little did I know that hell was around the corner.

9

CYPRUS HELL

SOMETIMES IN life you can find yourself in a situation that seems like a bad dream and you genuinely cannot believe what is happening to you. It is rare to feel like that, I know. Some people may be fortunate enough never to have found themselves in such a position. Not me.

I could probably write an entire book about what I went through in Cyprus in the summer of 2005. On the other hand, I can also sum it up in two words: pure hell. What was meant to be a holiday turned into a nightmare, although even when I think back to it now, more than three years on, the word nightmare barely does the episode justice.

Some background is necessary before we get to the gory details. It was not long after I returned from the British Lions tour to New Zealand, and I had just come through what had been one hell of a season. We had won the Grand Slam, which was amazing, of course, but the Lions experience had turned sour. I had been on the rugby treadmill for a very long time. I'd toured Argentina with Wales in the summer of 2004 and gone through a full season with the Ospreys and Wales. To be blunt about it, I was desperate for a break in the sunshine and the chance to switch off from rugby for a couple of weeks. Therefore, when

Dean and my mates Gavin Lewis and Ian Thomas saw a good late deal to Cyprus for two weeks, it seemed perfect.

Whenever I go on holiday, it has to be for a fortnight. Any less and I don't feel I have truly got away. If I go for a week, I am straight back into training on my return or somebody will want me to do something, and the bottom line is that I don't feel I have been away in the first place.

Anyway, up to the morning we were due to leave our hotel, the holiday was brilliant. It was one of the best I have ever been on for no other reason than the fact that I had managed to relax 100 per cent from start to finish. We'd had a few nights out – nothing over the top, just a meal and a few drinks – and had spent many a day just lounging around in the sun. The hotel was great. We were on half board, and although it was in Ayia Napa, a notoriously boisterous resort, we were outside the main hub and were able to take it easy in a bit of peace and quiet. The weather was great – there had barely been a cloud in the sky – and we had met a few Welsh people and palled up with them, spending a lot of time with a bunch of lads from Cardiff who were good company.

Gavin went home after a week, leaving just the three of us, but we carried on having a superb time, and when it was time to go, I remember thinking that I could have done with staying on a few days longer. Little did I know that I was to get my wish, only under circumstances that would stay with me for the rest of my life.

On the day of our departure, Dean and Ian were standing down in the hotel lobby with our cases ready to catch the bus that was laid on to take us to the airport – I was sitting out by the pool getting some last-minute rays – when out of nowhere a policeman and another guy came through the hotel door. They began talking to Dean in Greek, and he obviously didn't have a clue what they were saying, though he understood just enough to know that they wanted our passports, which the boys handed over. Dean came and got me from by the pool, saying something was clearly wrong – before long, that became even more apparent.

As these blokes jabbered away in Greek, time was getting on, and I was anxious that we had a plane to catch in about two hours. I told them this, but they didn't care, and before we knew it we were being shepherded into a police car and driven away, still not having a clue what all this was about.

By the time we reached the police station, it was an hour until our plane was due to take off, and I was really worried. I went up to the reception desk and spelled it out to the guy behind it that this was unacceptable and that we really had to go. He got up, put his hands on both my shoulders and pushed me down on to a chair, telling me that we weren't going anywhere. It was then I realised that this wasn't some unfortunate misunderstanding that was soon going to be sorted out; it was very serious, and the worst part of it was that we were still totally in the dark about what we were supposed to have done.

I asked to phone a lawyer, and they said that they would get one for me, but it was two hours before he turned up. During that time, we missed our flight and were starting to panic. Every time we pleaded for answers, we were given abuse and physically forced to sit down.

Finally, they let us know what we were supposed to have done. The lawyer explained that a bunch of youngsters had been walking home after a night out in Ayia Napa when a taxi had driven up. The driver had blown his horn, signalling for them to clear the road. Apparently, they had then jumped all over the bonnet of his car, and when he got out and complained, he had been hit to the ground and knocked unconscious. This had happened a full 11 days earlier, but the driver had supposedly recognised one of us as we walked into our hotel and believed us to be responsible.

Even at that early stage, it sounded like a load of bull. The one thing we knew for certain was that we hadn't been involved in the incident. We knew absolutely nothing about it. I took some relief from this at first, because I believed the truth would come out eventually. We had done nothing, and they had no proper evidence, so how could this possibly go any further? My relief didn't last.

Moments later, another policeman appeared to inform us that we were being charged with grievous bodily harm. We looked at each other, and I thought, 'This can't be happening.' Our Cypriot legal eagle was no help. He just kept telling us how long a stretch in prison we would be looking at if found guilty. And what he said made the colour drain from my face. If the charge was made to stick, we could expect to spend seven years in jail. 'But we haven't done this!' we cried. It made no difference.

'This man has cuts on his face,' said the lawyer.

'Look,' I said, 'we are not denying he has had a beating, but it wasn't us. We haven't a clue what all this is about.' Again, I was wasting my breath. Nothing we were saying was getting through.

By then, the situation was playing with my mind. On the one hand, I was convinced that it would be sorted out soon enough; on the other hand, if it had got this far without a shred of evidence being offered up, then who was to say where it might end?

I managed to stay outwardly calm, but my insides were churning up. Poor Ian struggled, though. He had a young son back at home, and he feared that he might miss out on seeing him grow up. That was how far this business had moved on – we were by then starting to think that we were going to jail for a long time for something we hadn't done.

We were still in a state of utter confusion. But it got worse. That night they split us up and carted us off to separate police stations, with me being sent off to Larnaca. I spent the whole night locked in a cell, but it was not any old cell. It was a real Bangkok Hilton style affair. It was no more than ten feet by six feet, with a stinking hole in the ground for a toilet. Above it was a shower, so you were expected to wash yourself while standing astride what was basically a shit-pit. There were cockroaches everywhere. I was given water, but it looked as though it had been left there for days and was warm. I had no choice but to drink it because it was all I had. There was also a blanket in one of the corners of the cell that looked as though somebody had peed all over it. I spent 36 hours in there. It was horrendous, like something out of a film.

I later found out that Dean and Ian were put in the same cell at another station, so they at least had each other for company. While I'm not saying for a minute that I went through anything worse than they did, I was left alone in torment for what seemed like an eternity. There were times when I even started to doubt myself. Because this had come so far, I began to question in my own mind whether something had actually happened that I had somehow forgotten about. Had I done something? Had I been somewhere close to this incident and not realised it at the time? But no, I had no recollection at all because it was simply a case of mistaken identity.

But how had it happened? I just could not stop asking myself that question over and over again. It turned into the longest 36 hours of my life, 36 hours in which I was awake the whole time. As the time passed, I began to resemble a zombie.

I kept asking the guards for a phone call. I wanted to contact the British Embassy, because I had visions of being left in the cell to rot. When I was eventually allowed to make a call, I got through to the rep of the holiday company we had travelled with, and he put me on to the embassy. They said that they would send someone out in a couple of hours, but it was a while longer than that before they got there.

In the meantime, the guards played mind games with me. It started when they tapped the cell door and said that there was a taxi ready to take me away. 'Taxi for Senator!' they yelled, Senator being the name of the hotel I had stayed at. My spirits soared, as I thought that it was finally all over; finally they had wised-up; finally someone had managed to get the message through to them that they had the wrong guys. But, of course, there was no taxi.

An hour passed. I thought that there must be some delay over paperwork, when again the call went up: 'Taxi for Senator!' Again, nothing. It slowly dawned on me that the bastards were just winding me up. I slid down a wall and sat in despair.

But they didn't let up. 'That man you beat up, he from this village,' they shouted. It appeared that they considered this assault as an affront to their community as well as the victim himself.

By that stage, my head was blown, but I was eventually let out of that hell-hole of a cell. I was taken in a police car to pick my brother and Ian up, and we were then dropped off back at the hotel. But that was by no means the end of it. They kept our passports and gave us strict orders to appear in court the next morning.

We looked at each other in disbelief, as if each of us wanted the other two to provide some answers. But none of us could. My brother and I worked out that we had indeed been out on the night in question, but we also ascertained that we were back at a reasonable hour, not long after midnight and hours before the attack on the taxi driver was supposed to have taken place. Ian had separated from us and gone drinking with other mates, and we asked him whether he was absolutely certain that he hadn't got involved in bother of any description. He was adamant that nothing had happened. So the confusion continued.

At least we could wash, eat and drink something decent, and get some sleep. The hotel let us have the rooms for two days, but after that we had to move around to wherever there were vacancies, because, of course, we had nothing booked.

In the meantime, I was able to phone home and speak to my mother and Mike Cuddy at the Ospreys, who arranged for a solicitor by the name of John Morris to come out and help us. At least we now had someone who could speak English and a means of talking to somebody who could actually let us know what the hell was going on.

We went back and forth to court every morning, but they didn't allow us to give any evidence. They just kept telling us that the case was being adjourned. On the first day we went to court with John, there had been a meeting before we got there, and we were told that the driver was willing to drop all charges if we paid him £30,000 – and that was in Cypriot pounds, so we were talking nearer £40,000 in sterling. John asked us first to be absolutely truthful with him. 'Boys, be straight with me,' he said. 'Have you done this?' We assured him that it was all nonsense, so he sent a message back to the Cypriots that there was no way they would be getting a penny from us, although I have to say that I was very close to agreeing to pay, because by that time I just wanted to get out of there. I was tired of shitting myself about what was going to happen to us all.

We were having a horrendous time. Ian had been very ill with a sickness bug – no surprise when you consider the state of that prison cell – and I was off my food, all caused by the tremendous amount of worry we were going through. The worst thing was that we appeared not to be getting anywhere for so long. We kept being told by the driver's lawyer that if we were lying, we were looking at all these years in jail. John was doing his best for us, but we were hitting brick walls. It got to the stage that we were all but resigned to not going home.

However, we did think of something that we hoped might help. Dean and I knew that we had returned to the hotel by the time of the incident, and we reckoned that we were bound to be on the hotel's CCTV footage somewhere. If we were, we were off the hook. So we trawled through tapes, and, sure enough, Dean was caught on camera going to reception to ask for his room key about three or four minutes before 2.30 a.m., the time the police had said the attack happened. As the incident had taken place about a mile and a half away from the hotel, it was a no-brainer. That would at least clear my brother, we thought, and as the taxi driver had from the start been pointing the finger at 'these three', we hoped it would mark an end of it for all of us.

To our dismay, the court wasn't interested at first. But our discovery did make a difference, because the taxi driver slowly started to realise that we had indeed been stitched up. It said it all that his financial demands were decreasing every day, until by the final day he wanted only £2,000. But John's insistence that we held firm on the money was the right call. Eventually, our CCTV detective work was seen by the judge, and the case was thrown out. That was it, all over at last.

About two days before the final court hearing, Dean and I really believed that we were going to jail, so Dean wanted our mother to come out and be with us. I wanted Gail with me as well. Gail, who is now my wife, and I had been on and off as a couple, and we were not officially together at that stage. I had been speaking to her on the phone throughout the ordeal, and even though she wasn't my partner at the time, she was a rock when I needed her most. I wanted somebody whom I knew I could depend on to be at my side if I was going to be locked up for a long time.

So my mother and Gail flew out, arriving the night before the final hearing. We didn't know which way it was going to go. We were either going to need our toothbrushes or we would be out afterwards celebrating. Thankfully, it went our way in the end. We had an interpreter in court who we didn't understand that well, but we knew well enough that the taxi driver's story sounded ridiculous and contained a whole host of contradictions. I was doing my nut by the end, just wanting to know the outcome. I couldn't take any more.

Mercifully, common sense prevailed, as it finally emerged that the accusations were complete nonsense. When it was finally over, the taxi driver received a rollicking from the judge for wasting everybody's time, and as we walked out of court, Dean wanted to kill him. I more or less had to hold him back. In the end, we just had to hope that he got everything he deserved, and while it wasn't much consolation, at least he looked ashamed of himself.

The taxi driver was just your average joe. I probably wouldn't recognise him if I walked past him in the street tomorrow. But for an average joe, he didn't half cause some trouble. I'm not the type of person who hates others easily. To me, hate is a strong word that should not be used lightly. But I can honestly say that I genuinely hate this man. His actions were unforgivable, motivated by financial greed, and he very nearly ruined not just our three lives, but countless others in the process – and all for nothing.

When we left the court, people from the prosecution side tried to apologise to us, but we weren't interested. Things had gone way too far for that.

That night, we went out for a meal, but we didn't celebrate wildly – we were just quietly relieved. We were also exhausted. The whole business had been terribly draining, mentally and physically.

To this day, I cannot get over what happened. I cannot for the life of me understand how something like that can go so far with no evidence other than the say-so of one taxi driver. It's frightening and quite honestly enough to put you off going abroad for good. I would like to think that it was a one-off. I have not heard too many stories like that, and I have been back to Cyprus since, because I have property interests out there. But each time I go back, I sit in the departure lounge in the airport ready to come home, praying that nobody taps me on the shoulder and counting the minutes to take-off.

In short, it was the worst week and a half of my life, and the other depressing little footnote was that the whole episode cost me £11,000, because Dean and Ian had spent out by the time the original holiday had finished, and I had to pay all our accommodation and living costs for the extra time we were there. Not that I really cared about that. In fact, money seemed trivial after what we had gone through.

And I suppose there was one good thing that came out of it – I now saw Gail in a whole new light. I had always cared for her, but the support she gave me throughout that horrible time convinced me that I loved her and wanted to spend the rest of my life with her. I realised just how much I depended on her, and I thought back to how I had felt when she had arrived in Cyprus the night before our D-Day in court – like a weight had been lifted off my shoulders, even though there were still no guarantees about what was going to happen. She was willing to fly out and help me, even though we weren't together at the time and I could still be going to jail. It made me realise that she would do anything for me.

Gail went to a different school from me, in Ystlyfera, on the other side of the valley, so I didn't know her during my schooldays. I was 18 and working for the window company when I first saw her. We were doing the house next door to hers. Her brother Andrew and her sister Donna were in school with me, and I had heard a lot of people talking about Gail, saying how smart she was, but I thought nothing of it.

When I spotted her for the first time, I realised that she must be the girl I had heard so much about. I was attracted to her straight away, but nothing happened. I was way too shy to even have considered approaching her, and, besides, I had never been the type of lad who was obsessed with girls like some of my mates were.

Gail was quite something, though, with long, curly, blonde hair, and I knew it would be a real result if I could ever get to go out with her. Then came the works Christmas party of 1995, and Gail just so happened to be in the same pub as we were at the end of the night. I was totally drunk and told her how I felt about her. When I woke up the next morning, I was hung-over and felt like a right idiot. But I'd obviously made an impression, because a couple of days later she phoned me at my grandmother's house. She was at a phone box about a mile down the road. I sprinted down to meet her, and we just went from there.

We were together on and off, like many couples are. We were young – Gail was 17 when we first got together, and I was 19 – so we had some difficult times. We finished for a year and a half about seven years ago and completely went our separate ways.

When my rugby took off, Gail found it difficult. All of a sudden, I was getting a lot of attention, and I probably changed a little bit. I started to enjoy my stardom a little too much, and the nature of what I was doing meant I spent a lot of time away. I was getting attention from everyone, and that didn't help us.

We always remained friends, but we got back together in 2005 after Cyprus. Gail was with me before any of my rugby success and has always been loving and loyal. She is still the same person she always was. She doesn't know the first thing about rugby, and she doesn't want to, but that's fine by me.

Even when we weren't together, she was there for me, and that means a hell of a lot. We have been through so much, and Gail knows all there is to know about me. We have had rows, really bad rows, when we have said terrible things to one another on the spur of the moment. But when you can talk about it and move on, then you become stronger.

When we got home from Cyprus, we sorted a few things out and decided to get back together. Later that year, on 23 December, we were married. We had been together on and off for so long, but it felt right to make the commitment at that time. I proposed in November, and it then happened very quickly, us tying the knot at our local church, Christ Church, in Garnant, and having our bash at Craig-y-Nos castle in Abercraig, which is supposedly haunted. Maybe it was a fitting place to get hitched.

It was a lovely day. Dean and my mate Barry Windsor were best men, and the evening at Craig-y-Nos was really beautiful. All the Christmas decorations were up, and we filled the place with friends and family. To get everyone together for such a perfect day meant the world to me, especially after the year I had been through. I know life is about ups and downs, but that year was quite something. I had the highs of a Grand Slam, becoming a British Lion and getting married, and also the low of Cyprus. It was just crazy, and I suppose getting married in a haunted castle was some way to end a year I will never forget.

10

GARETH JENKINS AND THE 2007 WORLD CUP

WHO CAN blame any Welsh rugby fan for regarding the 2007 World Cup as one of the blackest events in the history of our game? In fact, the entire year was one of bitter frustration for most of the players. In terms of the end result, it was admittedly a real low point, but I'll say now that I do not go along with the negative perception of the coaching duo in charge at the time, Gareth Jenkins and Nigel Davies. Some supporters and pundits have been scathing about the supposed failures of Gareth and Nigel, but I do not share their outlook. I'll call it as I see it – and I saw it differently.

The summer before the World Cup, I took the chance to have a couple of operations that were long overdue – one on my right shoulder, the other on my left elbow. If I was ever going to have them done, it had to be during the pre-season so as to give me as much time as possible to recover and to miss as little action as possible.

I said nothing publicly at the time, but there was a small risk in having the surgeries. There is never a 100 per cent guarantee of success when you go under the knife, I know. The shoulder op was the more straightforward of the two – just a case of cleaning the joint out, as I'd had a series of niggling problems with it. However, the problem with my elbow was more unusual and was where the uncertainty lay.

There was nerve damage in the joint from the accident I'd had a couple of years earlier when I had come off my bike. At first, the injury didn't cause me any trouble, but gradually it got worse. It was bothering me more and more, and I began to get pins and needles during games. I then started to get cramps in my hand, and it even got to the point that my fist would involuntarily clench up as I was walking down the street.

That was when I decided enough was enough. I couldn't put up with that in my line of work, so I resigned myself to the surgery. But my surgeon, Jeff Graham, warned me that there was a slim possibility that I would lose the movement and control of some of my fingers. 'It's a slim chance,' he said, 'but I have to tell you anyway.' If that had happened, it would have meant the end of my rugby career. How could I have gone on as a professional without full control of my hand? Perhaps I could have tried taping my fingers together. I don't think so, somehow. I knew I had to put my livelihood in Jeff's hands. Thankfully, though, it went well, and I bounced back fairly quickly.

I was out for about a month to six weeks all told, and it did set me back a bit in terms of fitness. Any player will tell you that it is extremely frustrating having to watch teammates go through a summer programme of conditioning when you can't take part. But it just meant that I had to work that little bit harder when I did get the go-ahead from the medics.

As it turned out, things ended up going really well. I eventually felt fitter than I had done for a long time, after getting through a hell of a lot of work on my speed, general fitness and strength – some off my own bat, the rest with the Ospreys fitness man Huw Bevan and Mark Bennett of Wales. That pleased me, because it was a big season coming up. Going into the World Cup, I knew that I was as fit, as fast and as strong as I had ever been, because we were all scientifically tested.

In some ways, my enforced break had actually worked in my favour, because I had caught up with the rest of the lads but at the same time felt fresh in a way that I perhaps wouldn't have in normal circumstances. The World Cup had given me the motivation and determination to get fit and enabled me to make progress working on my own.

Contrary to what some people might believe, the atmosphere in the Wales camp going into the 2007 tournament was good. At least that was the way I saw it. The one thing you have to say about Gareth and Nigel is that they are genuinely nice guys and always approachable. Some of the training sessions did drag on too long and some were, the players felt, overly physical. But there were meetings between the coaching staff and the senior players in which things were discussed and subsequently changed, and, to me, everything was relatively harmonious as the big kick-off in France approached.

You learn from every coach you work with, and I thought Gareth and Nigel were good. I worked more closely with Nigel, of course, being a back, as Gareth was more heavily involved with the forwards, but I took things from both of them. What I loved about the two of them was that they believed in my ability and what I could offer the team. They gave me licence to express myself. They urged me to try things and not to worry if I made a mistake, telling me that I would get it right the next time. That's the way I like to work. That's the attitude that gives me confidence. There are not too many coaches around who are like that.

That said, the two of them, Gareth in particular, were always going to be judged on what happened at the World Cup –

although I thought that Gareth was harshly dealt with when it came down to it. Others were responsible for what happened – by that I mean us players. We let ourselves down on the field, and we should certainly not have lost the match against Fiji – not in a month of Sundays. We should not have conceded the tries we conceded against them. That is the hardest thing to stomach about the whole episode.

Because of my injury, I missed the England and Argentina warm-up matches in August 2007, although I probably could have got through the match against the Pumas at a push. Scarcely anyone in Wales will need reminding of the 62–5 thrashing we suffered at Twickenham, a match I watched on my own in my front room at home. I'm not a good spectator at the best of times. I have watched Wales games in a variety of places, including in pubs, and it gets on my nerves. The worst thing is having to listen to people's comments about the way the team is playing that make you want to poke them in the eye.

That day, I chose not to travel to London with the rest of the boys. There was no way I wanted to sit in the stands. That's not my scene at all. I was biting my nails enough watching the match at home, though at least there I could analyse the game in my own way. I like to make my own mind up on matches if I am not playing, rather than be forced to listen to the opinions of the thousands of 'coaches' we have in Wales.

As it turned out, Twickenham was not the best day for us. It was a depressing game to watch, and the worst thing about it was that there appeared to be no spirit in the way we played. The performance led to hysteria among some members of the press, and while some of the criticism was a little misinformed, we didn't really have a leg to stand on – we had to take it.

Gareth and Nigel didn't want to risk me in the Argentina game a fortnight later, and they weren't even 100 per cent sure about giving me the green light to face the French a week after that. But I thought that I really needed a game under my belt before the World Cup. The French beat us convincingly, 34–7, and there were all kinds of 'men against boys' lines in the papers. It was annoying, but at least I felt encouraged from a personal standpoint. My fitness had stood up well, and I felt fresh and sharp at an important time. I had been clocking 4.66 seconds over 40 metres in training and lifting heavier weights than I had ever lifted. As we prepared to leave for our base near La Baule, I was convinced that I was about to have a very good World Cup, and not just me, but the team, too. I genuinely thought that.

I was happy with the free role I was given in the game plan as well. The aim was to get the ball in my hands as often as possible, and I didn't feel too restricted by a rigid structure. I thought that this was perfect for what I could offer. It has since become plain that others in the squad felt differently. A couple of the guys have since gone public, saying that they felt confused about the game plan under Gareth and Nigel and that they really weren't happy at all with the set-up. I wouldn't knock them for that, because we're all entitled to our viewpoint, but what can I say? I just didn't pick up on that at the time. Perhaps I was too wrapped up in the work I was trying to do.

I was happy. Yes, there was confusion at times about how we were going to approach some games, but, to a large extent, I would put that down to the high number of senior players who were in the squad. We were always encouraged to have an input, but at some stages there were a huge number of ideas being thrown into the pot – differing opinions about what was the best way forward, the best formula to beat a certain side. Senior players would go into meetings with management and say 'We need to be doing more of this, and less of this.' Their opinions would be taken on board, and then the management team would say what they wanted to happen. And that did get confusing, because half the time you ended up wondering to yourself, 'Well, just what have we agreed to do here?' On one or two occasions, there might just have been too many ideas being put forward, too many voices being heard. Yet I never got hung up about it at the time. I never fretted that it was a real problem that was going to fatally undermine what we were trying to do.

This confusion was certainly no excuse for what we produced on the field. We were grown-up enough, experienced enough, to have got the job done against a side such as Fiji. That's why there has not been any attempt by the boys to deflect the blame since. We genuinely believed that we had let ourselves down in failing to reach the quarter-finals, yet we always knew that when it came down to it, it was Gareth who was going to bear the brunt of our failure. But the manner in which he was asked to leave – virtually straight after the defeat to Fiji and before we had even left camp in La Baule – disappointed me.

In the immediate aftermath of the loss, I made a personal pledge to myself to front up to as many requests to speak to the media as possible. I knew Gareth and Nigel were going to cop it big time, but I didn't want them to be on their own, so I made a point of doing a few interviews straight away, emphasising that it was the players who had lost the game. The point I wanted to put out was that no matter what structure we had adopted going into the match, we should never have lost to the Fijians.

The only thing to admire that day was the achievement of Gareth Thomas in winning his 100th cap, although I know that the circumstances ruined it for him. That was criminal, because such a great player deserved a better occasion. Alfie's had his ups and downs. He's had his selection heartaches, especially under Graham Henry, but he's always come back stronger. For me, the sign of a truly great player is one who can perform at a world-class level in a number of different positions. That's Alfie. Skills-wise he is up there with the best, but he's also strong and never shies out of anything, even when he's bruised, battered, cut and bleeding.

People ask me who are the best players I have played alongside, and Alfie is always one of the first I mention. Had he not had his spell out of favour under Henry, who knows how many caps he might have won. His life has read like a soap opera at times, but we should never forget what a great captain he was. I have never known someone be such a nutcase off the field and yet so inspirational as a leader on it. Alfie doesn't take life too seriously, but he takes his rugby extremely seriously. He will be remembered in our game for ever – for his ability and for his personality.

After the Fiji match, if I'm honest, we all knew that Gareth Jenkins' days were over, even shortly after the final whistle. You could just sense it in the atmosphere. We'd all been around long enough and knew how things worked in Wales. Gareth had had it, and there was no getting away from that. Coaches in Wales are either messiahs or they are out on their arses, end of story.

After the game, we went to listen to the speeches in the marquees by the ground, but we made our way back to our hotel as soon as we could. The mood was horrible as we headed back to our base, about an hour's drive west of Nantes. A good deal of the boys just wanted to drown their sorrows, but all the while you couldn't get away from the sense that something final was going to happen.

If we expected something momentous, though, we didn't expect it to happen the following morning. Gareth came in to see the boys, who were gathered in a room, and said that he wished us well for the future but that he would no longer be coaching us. The lads all felt that it could have been dealt with better, and to watch a proud man such as Gareth have to confront us like that totally demoralised me.

The situation was surreal. Gareth was forced to board the bus to the airport, knowing that his authority was gone, and I don't know about the other lads, but I found that very hard to deal with. I was upset enough that we were out of the World Cup, but I was also upset for Gareth. My heart went out to him.

To this day, I have a real regard for Gareth Jenkins, a real respect for him that will never diminish. It's not just what he did for Llanelli and the Scarlets; it's the passion and effort that he puts into his work. Gareth is one of the most passionate men I have ever met. Rugby is his life, and that is why what happened to him as coach of Wales would have been tremendously difficult for him to take. It was hard enough for the players to take.

When he took the national job, he was the logical choice because of what he had achieved over such a long period of time at Stradey Park, and I suppose it's one of life's cruel twists that it never worked out for him in the one role he always craved. I never had much to do with him before he took the Wales job, simply because I never played at Stradey, but in the short time I did work with him he became a friend as well as a colleague – or should I say boss?

I went to a Labour Party dinner with Gareth and Martyn Williams at Wembley Stadium in 2007. We spent the whole day together – and what a day it was. I have always found Gareth to be a really top guy, someone you could speak to about anything – not just rugby, but anything. He is well read and seems to know at least a little bit about most issues. But he was a legend that day. The dinner was to commemorate ten years of sport since Labour took power under Tony Blair in 1997, and there were a whole host of famous people there, not just politicians such as

Blair and Gordon Brown, but also big names such as Sir Alex Ferguson and Mick Hucknall.

Socially, Gareth Jenkins is one of the best people you could wish to go out with. He will speak to absolutely everyone, no matter how big their profile is. One of the first people we bumped into that afternoon was Tony Blair himself, who was introduced to us by Alastair Campbell, whom we all knew from the 2005 Lions tour when he had travelled as the squad's media manager. Tony Blair spoke to me and Martyn, and as we were conscious of minding our p's and q's, we kept our answers brief and quite bland, but Gareth was different and really began chirping up. The first words out of his mouth were, 'Hi, Tony, I'm Gareth Jenkins. Well, a tough ten years, Tony, a tough ten years . . .' as if he was talking to a guy over his garden fence. The follow-up was priceless: 'Are you bringing out a book, Tony?' Martyn and I looked at each other in amazement.

Next up was Gordon Brown. As the soon-to-be prime minister came over, Gareth piped up with, 'Hi, Gordon. You like your rugby, don't you? You used to play, didn't you? Got kicked in the head, didn't you?' You could see that Gordon Brown was taken aback, as he had probably never been spoken to like that before in such circumstances. I think Gareth was referring to him having lost an eye as the result of an old rugby injury, but Brown didn't seem to mind.

As soon as Gareth started speaking to someone, Martyn and I would at first cringe. But when we saw the reaction he got, we had to laugh and admire him. He was incredible, and people couldn't get enough of him. Looking back, it was brilliant the way he was able to relate to those people. Gareth was on fire that day, and everyone loved him. I don't think a lot of the people there had met anyone like him before.

Gareth is one of the best man-managers I have ever

encountered. He will do anything for you, and is one of the nicest guys I have ever met. He is a people person, one of the best in that respect. I guarantee you would love to have a night out with him.

Later on, we were involved in an auction in which Martyn, Gareth and I ended up onstage with Sir Alex Ferguson on behalf of the WRU and Manchester United. People were bidding for a day at training with Wales or United followed by a dinner afterwards. The money flying about was mad, although there was a bit of a difference in price between the two options on offer. In the end, a day with us went for something like £27,000 and with United it was £75,000. I felt like saying to the winner that they could probably just have turned up at Sophia Gardens one day and watched us train for nothing, but I thought I'd better not.

We spoke briefly to Sir Alex. He was really enjoying himself. To be honest, Martyn and I spent the whole event in awe, spotting celebrities, nudging each other and saying, 'Look who's over there!' We chatted to Barry Gibb from the Bee Gees and Mick Hucknall, too, a few beers giving us a bit more confidence as the day wore on. I was mindful that my testimonial year was coming up and asked Mick's manager what it would cost for the singer to perform at one of our functions. The starting figure I was quoted was £200,000. 'OK, thanks,' I said. 'I'll get back to you.' It was just a brilliant day.

I don't mind admitting that I got quite close to Gareth, and it disturbed me that he disappeared from the scene for a while after leaving the Wales post. He has since gone back to work for the Scarlets in a development role away from pure coaching, and I'm sure he'll do wonders. He is certainly one of the biggest names in Welsh rugby, and it would have been a real shame if he had not bounced back. What happened with Wales must have knocked him for six, but he is resilient, and I am not surprised to see him back in the game where he belongs.

I enjoyed the experience of the 2007 World Cup despite the way it turned out. It was my second tournament, and the environment we worked in was good for me. You can never get away from the fact that you are playing at a World Cup, which is a privilege and a great opportunity.

Why didn't it work out for us? Who knows? How can you explain the fact that a Welsh team that comprised the same players flopped at the World Cup one minute and then within a matter of months won the Grand Slam?

The real problem for Gareth Jenkins was that the team never really performed at any stage of the 16 months or so that he was in charge. It wasn't just at the World Cup that we were poor; we didn't play well during the Six Nations that went before it. I missed the opening two matches through injury and watched the boys lose both of them, narrowly at home to Ireland in the opener followed by a desperately disappointing defeat to Scotland at Murrayfield.

What happened was basically the opposite of what we went through in 2008. Instead of getting off to a winning start and building momentum, we began badly and struggled to get out of the rut. In particular, the Scotland match was awful – we lost 21–3 but barely ever threatened to score a try.

Our mindset could not have been more different back then. We didn't have the mental strength that we have now. We were crying out for a win to build something on. However, we weren't helped by an unfortunate little footnote to events in Edinburgh. I wasn't on the trip, but a group of the lads went to a bar in the city after the game for a few drinks – and it was a move that backfired.

Contrary to what some people might believe, it was never a

case of the lads not caring about the loss earlier in the day. Win or lose, players sometimes need to unwind with a few drinks after a match. If you go to your room after a bad reverse and just sit there, you can end up torturing yourself by running through all the mistakes you made. It can actually do you good to get out and forget about it for a while until it's back to work on the analysis the following day. But once you are out and about, you cannot predict what sort of situation is going to unfold, and if you get involved in something, it can be impossible to get out of it.

While in the bar, some of the boys took some pretty vociferous criticism from Wales fans who were also there – not for being out, but for the way they had played that day. I know that my Ospreys teammate Jonathan Thomas was on the receiving end of some pretty strong stuff. Sometimes, you can take it on the chin, but at other times it can get so rude, so vicious, so personal, that you cannot help but bite back. Apparently, that's what happened on that occasion. It came to a point that the abusive fans had to be told to leave by the bar staff.

I'm glad I wasn't there, to be truthful. I have taken some stick in my time. For example, I've had someone come up to me in an airport and say 'Thanks for ruining my weekend' as we returned home from a Wales away match. 'I've wasted hundreds of pounds coming here just to watch that shower of shit.' Often, the sort of person who will shout at you will be in a crowd. Of course, this makes them a hero among their mates, but it can be difficult to accept.

When we were thrashed by Ireland in Dublin in 2002, we arrived at Dublin Airport the following morning and were roundly booed by the Wales fans travelling home. We had to run the gauntlet right through the middle of them to the main checkout. We were literally booed onto the plane. It was horrendous, and it had a real effect on me. And it didn't stop at the terminal, either. Even on the aircraft, fans were coming out with really graphic and loud abuse: 'Fucking disgusting', 'Nobody tried', 'You were shit', 'You'll be dropped next week', 'None of you give a fuck'. As I sat there through the abuse, I was convinced that it would be the lowest point of my career, and I was desperate to get home to the privacy of my own house.

Nobody needs to tell me that paying punters are entitled to express their views, but I cannot see how people can be so filled with hate at times. I know I wouldn't be like that if I was in their shoes.

I came back for the third leg of the 2007 tournament, against France away. That match typified our fragile state of mind. We caught the French cold with a blistering start, scoring tries through Tom Shanklin and Alix Popham, but the mind games then kicked in. We just weren't used to being in that position against such a good side away from home, and it was as if we panicked, as if we thought that we weren't really allowed to be winning in Paris. I felt that we were actually asking ourselves why we were in the lead. Needless to say, it wasn't long before the momentum shifted to France, and by the time Jamie Robinson ran in a try well into the second half, we were all but out of contention and in damage-limitation mode.

Still the elusive victory wouldn't arrive, not even when we travelled to face Italy in Rome two weeks later for a match that will always be remembered for a farcical finish. I had scored a try in the first half, but, again, we just couldn't get any patterns going. As usual, Italy were doing a great job of spoiling things for us, but instead of wearing them down and imposing our game plan on them, as we did in 2008, we weren't able to find a way to break the pattern of the match. We just didn't have the nous or the sheer grit to overcome them.

With seconds to go, and us trailing 23–20, James Hook planted a penalty that was in easy range of the posts into touch because we had been told by Chris White, the referee, that we had time to take the lineout and go for the try. But there were obviously some crossed wires somewhere, because no sooner had Hooky put the ball out than White blew for full-time. There were all sorts of protests from our guys but no way of going back. We'd lost in Rome again and were heading for a Six Nations whitewash. The incident was yet another example of how nothing was going right for us at that time. If ever a team needed the gods to smile on them, it was us, but instead it seemed as though we were cursed.

But I don't dwell too much on that episode. In my view, it wouldn't have made any difference to the overall picture if we had gone for goal and got a 23–23 draw. The public back in Wales would still have seen the draw as a disaster, and we would still have been pilloried. The one thing a draw would have meant was that we weren't playing England to avoid total humiliation the following week, but it scarcely mattered in real terms.

The performance at home in the final game was our best of the tournament. Although to lose five out of five matches would have been awful, there was no real pressure on us. We just went out and played. Perhaps if we had thought like that earlier, we would have been more successful.

Our forwards really roughed the English pack up that day, and we notched a 28–17 victory, but we'd long since moved on from the old attitude of 'as long as we beat the English . . .' And, to be honest, the win did little to restore faith in the side among the press or the public. Gareth remained under pressure, but he insisted that he should be judged on the World Cup, which, of course, he was.

11

TROUBLE OFF THE PITCH

IN THE nine years or so that I have played for Wales, I have learned that people are fickle. One minute you're the greatest thing the game has ever seen, the next you're coming under a hail of criticism.

As far as the press is concerned, I haven't done too badly in my time. I've had my critics, certainly, but I've been given a pretty fair ride. But that doesn't mean that I haven't been hurt by some of the things that have been written or said about me. It does hurt, and anyone who says different is lying.

When I first started playing for Neath in televised games, I found that people were not afraid to let me know if I had made a couple of mistakes. And I don't just mean journalists; I'm talking about members of the public, as well. Down the years, I have got into no end of scrapes, fights and arguments because of this.

I have had people I have never seen before come right up to me in the street or in the supermarket and say with real hostility etched on their faces, 'You're shit, you are.' I have been in bars and pubs and had things thrown at me simply because I had a bad game the previous weekend.

There is one incident that sticks in my mind. It was after a night out in Swansea with my brother and some friends shortly after I had broken into the Wales team back in 2000. It was very late, and we had made our way to the bus terminal in the centre of town to catch a minibus back to Ammanford. I must have had a bad game shortly before because all of a sudden there was some bloke shouting at me from the other side of the street, hurling abuse and basically telling me how crap I was.

Next, a beer bottle flew through the air and hit me on the head. It just bounced off, thank goodness, though not without cutting me by my eye. A scuffle broke out, and as there were quite a few police about, I ran over to them. The culprit was apprehended and ushered away. I don't know what happened to him. I can remember thinking at the time, 'What right do people have to act like that? What right do they have even to say something, never mind throw a bottle at me?'

Unfortunately, that was not an isolated incident. I have been attacked on numerous occasions – and for no reason. I've been grabbed hold of, punched in the face and hit on the back of the head – always by blokes I don't know and for no reason that I am aware of.

The situation was worst just after I had broken into the Wales squad. People would come up to me if I was out for an evening and sneer at me in an aggressive way, saying, 'Who the hell do you think you are?' They would accuse me of strutting around, of being arrogant, of being toffee-nosed, of looking down at people and of acting as if I owned the place.

That is just not me. It never has been. And people who really know me will confirm that. But it's no use. There have been times in my life when it has seemed as though everyone has thought that they can have a pop at me as and when the mood grabs them. And I am not the only one to suffer like this. I know for a fact that Gavin Henson has been through something similar.

Maybe at just five foot seven inches I have been seen as an easy target. Idiots are more ready to have a go at me than Ryan Jones or Ian Gough. Thankfully, though, I gradually learned to deal with this kind of thing as the years went by. I have walked away from hundreds of provocative situations in my time. I could easily have got involved in a hell of a lot more trouble if my attitude had been different.

However, there was one instance, just before the 2007 World Cup, when I didn't really have the chance to walk away. I'll give you some background first. My brother Dean is of a similar stature to me, he looks a bit like me and there are even times when he has been mistaken for me. He's a decent rugby player in his own right. He plays for Amman United, the club where I began, in Division Three West, and I enjoy going to watch him when I get the chance. Unfortunately, he gets abuse from people in the crowd just because he happens to be my brother. It's a way of trying to put him off his game. These days, I laugh when it happens, and he thinks it's funny now, too. But it wasn't like that when it first started. It used to upset me, and there are still times when Dean will lose his rag during a match if he gets stick for being my younger brother. I remember going to watch one game at Trimsaran, and the abuse he got from the line was pretty heavy. 'You're shit like your brother' was the gist of it.

Anyway, during the summer before the World Cup, we went to a fundraising dinner at the Amman Centre in Ammanford for an old school friend of mine called Paul Pugh, who was so badly beaten up that he will have to spend the rest of his life in a wheelchair. It was touch and go whether he would make it in the days immediately after the attack, and he is still receiving hospital treatment now. His cause is important to us, and we went out and enjoyed ourselves.

Our party included me, Gail, my brother and a few of our

friends. When the do finished, we started to walk home, which was only about a mile or so away. On the way, a bar was still open, even though it was gone midnight, so we decided to call in for another drink to finish off what had been a good night. Bad move. If I'd known what was to happen inside, I would have walked on by.

I went to the bar and ordered some drinks. The next thing I knew, we were being asked to leave. The trouble was that I had paid for the round. As we hadn't been served and weren't going to get the chance to drink our drinks, I asked for my money back. With that, I was grabbed from behind by two bouncers who started to physically throw me out. To this day, I have no idea what the problem was. When we arrived at the place, we knew that it was late, so we made absolutely certain with the people on the door that it was OK to go in, which they said it was.

Obviously, there was some misunderstanding, because before I knew it the bouncers were getting really shirty. To make matters worse, I had just had the operations on my shoulder and elbow; in fact, the surgery had been on the Tuesday and this was the Friday night, so both areas were still really tender. The last thing I needed was two heavies manhandling me, grabbing hold of me when one of my arms was in a sling and trying to throw me about.

I was fuming that I had somehow walked into a situation like that. I knew that if anything happened to either injury, it could mean an extra six to eight weeks out, or, heaven forbid, missing out on going to the World Cup altogether. But there was nothing I could do. There was a bit of minor scuffling as Dean and Gail argued with the bouncers, but nothing much happened. It was hardly anything, really, just a bit of pushing. I was in no fit state to fight anyone, my arms being virtually immobilised. Thankfully,

I left the place in one piece, with no additional damage done. That wasn't the end of it, though.

We walked out of the place and up the road. In the meantime, one of the bouncers made a complaint about me. Thinking about it now, it was an absolute joke, but there we were, my brother and I, being picked up in the street by the police and arrested for our part in a supposed bar brawl. I was livid about the whole business. If this had been just any old Joe Bloggs from down the road, nothing whatsoever would have come of it. But because of who I was, these people wanted to press charges. I knew we had done nothing wrong and that eventually the truth would out, but I could have done without it.

To add insult to injury, the next morning the incident was in the news. I could deal with that, even though it was embarrassing, but the effect I knew it would have on my family riled me. My grandfather Emrys wasn't well at the time, and I knew that it wouldn't help him. I also knew that my mother would be upset and that Gail was already upset. It's this inevitable knock-on effect that is tough to accept.

I then had to go through all the usual rigmarole with the police, who kept on telling me that I would have to report back to them at such and such a time. It was so frustrating, because I knew that nothing would come of it. We'd done nothing wrong. I asked the police to review the CCTV footage, because I knew that the camera would clear us. Lo and behold, after a few weeks of pointless hassle, I received a phone call from the police saying that the matter would not be taken any further. But that was only after my name had been dragged through the mud and my family put through a lot of anxiety. It really pissed me off.

Throughout my career, I have had to deal with troublemakers. It's not so bad these days, although that could be because I don't go out half as much as I used to. I have largely learned how to deal with them, and I know I am by no means in a unique position.

Most of the lads in the Ospreys team and the Wales squad enjoy a beer when the time is right. Don't we all? The important thing is doing it when the time is right and making sure that you work hard in between. There is nothing better than playing a good game, getting a good win and then having a few beers to celebrate, and I don't think you should knock professional players for doing that.

In my younger days, I went out almost every other week. I enjoyed my rugby and enjoyed my life, but I've cut back these days. The older you get, the harder it is to get away with it, but I will still go out after a good win. I think the importance of socialising in professional sport is sometimes underplayed. At the end of the day, that is how you really get to know your teammates, how you find out what makes them tick, what their personalities are and what their outlook on things is. That does matter when you are working with them every day.

After a good win, the Ospreys boys will sometimes go out together and celebrate in Swansea. However, on other occasions I'll just head home and go to my local football club, which is called the Fisherman's, or Amman United rugby club. I'm a homeboy when it comes down to it. I have never lived further than two miles away from where I grew up.

For all the trouble that has come my way because of who I am, there is the other side of the coin: the positive attention, even adulation, of people who admire what professional sportsmen do, whether they are ten-year-old kids or seventy-year-old grandmothers. When I first arrived on the scene at Neath, it was something that took me by surprise. I was just a local boy from Ammanford. I'd never had someone ask me for my autograph in my life, and it took me aback when it first happened, because I wasn't prepared for it.

When I broke into the Wales team, the whole business just amazed me. I had people on the phone asking me to do things, I had sponsors queuing up and, for a time, I had people I didn't know from Adam coming up to me in the street wanting to shake my hand. Young girls would even approach me and tell me that they or their friends fancied me. Older women did, too, and you know what? They were sometimes worse than the youngsters. I didn't know what the hell was going on, and I didn't know how to deal with it. If I had my time over again, I would want some training in how to handle the fame.

I also received fan mail, which was being sent to Neath Rugby Club in some volume. There were letters requesting autographs, letters from schools wanting me to do things, birthday cards, messages from girls and Valentine's Day cards. Companies wanted me to endorse their products, and rugby clubs wanted me to attend their functions and visit them to take training sessions. I loved going out and about to the clubs, and I still do. In fact, I'll be gutted when they stop asking me. It was just at that time it was all too much, too soon.

For example, it blew me away that someone wanted to offer me a car for nothing. But that's exactly what happened when I first became an international player. Toyota were willing to hand over the keys to a two-seater convertible sports model and update it every six months. I was speechless. I was also approached by Welsh Milk to appear in a series of TV ads. There I was on the box with a milk moustache before the weather bulletin. I cringe when I think about that now, and I remember thinking at the time, 'Where the hell has all this come from? This is mad.'

I was also given a free pair of Adidas boots, which struck a chord. If you ask any rugby player or footballer who grew up asking their mam and dad to buy them as expensive a pair of boots as they could afford what it feels like the first time a company actually gives you a pair, actually wants you to wear their product, they will tell you that it's one hell of a buzz. It was no different for me.

Before Adidas approached, I had been wearing a pair of Reeboks that I had been given by Roy, the groundsman at Neath. I had been bowled over when Roy had given them to me, but I'd worn them for about a year and a half, and they were fairly battered, so to get new Adidas boots was brilliant. These days, I wear Pumas, having signed a deal with them for the last couple of years, and they have been great. A good mate of mine called Mike Workman works for them, and they have helped me out a lot.

I know the other side, though. I've had times when nobody has been interested in providing me with so much as a pair of flip-flops. By the time I went to the World Cup in 2003, for example, the end of a spell of two years or so when I barely figured in the Welsh set-up, I was back to buying my own boots. Just before we set off for Australia, I remember going into JJB Sports in Swansea and buying myself two pairs of Nike boots – that's how things can go from one extreme to the other.

I did appoint an agent early on in my career, but that didn't help too much because people still approached me personally, and I inevitably ended up agreeing to do everything. The period when I was first making a name for myself was a great time and taught me how much the public wants to be associated with success – I was later to learn all about their fickleness. I know about it anyway from my own experience, because in the last decade I have been in pubs during Wales games – and actually slagged off Wales myself. It's mad, and I think it's definitely part of our culture.

All I would say to any youngster who is on the verge of making a breakthrough in professional sport is, 'Be prepared.' On the one hand, it is difficult becoming public property and having to listen to critics; on the other hand, there is nothing better than hearing someone say how good you are. The highs are fantastic, but you also have to cope with the lows.

You also get used to people staring at you in public. There are times when I can sense that someone is going to come over and ask me for an autograph a full ten seconds before they actually do. Don't get me wrong – it's a great feeling when that happens.

Not long after we won the Grand Slam under Warren Gatland, I popped along to one of my local shops in Ammanford to buy a new mobile phone. I only had a couple of minutes spare, as I had to shoot off somewhere – or at least that was the plan. I ended up spending over an hour at the place with loads of kids and people who were just walking past doing their shopping. They all wanted to stop and talk and have their photos taken with me. It was amazing.

If I am honest, it's madder now than it has ever been, but I have a far better idea of how to deal with it. I am older, wiser and have seen it all before, and, fortunately, in the last year or so I have had a pretty positive press.

My family play a part in keeping me sane, a big part, as do my friends, the majority of whom I have known since I was in primary school. Thank goodness none of them would ever dream of treating me any differently. They take the piss out of me relentlessly at times, but I take it all in good heart.

I haven't changed at all since I started playing rugby. I put the bins out and help around the house when I can, even though I'm not the best at certain things, in particular ironing, which I find especially difficult. I enjoy cooking, too, which I have had to master because of the amount of time I spend away from home. I can turn my hand to a proper dish if I have to, such as pasta, although when I am on tour I will take the easy option and eat out if I can. I'll try most things. I like pasta, chicken and steaks rather than fish, though with the Wales team I seem to always find myself in fish restaurants.

You need an escape from rugby at times, and I think all players should have at least one other hobby away from the sport. We live very close to a golf course in Garnant, and I play as much as I can. It's not easy, though, because of rugby and family commitments.

I love my life now. I am at a stage that I am becoming more of an out-and-out family man, and I certainly love spending time with my two-year-old daughter Georgie. She's a hobby in herself. She's absolutely nuts and really keeps me on my toes. She's amazing, a real handful who keeps me fit running after her. But I wouldn't have it any other way. Things have worked out perfectly for me.

My valley is a safe haven. I know everyone, and everyone knows me. To them, I am just Shane rather than Shane Williams the rugby player – and that's great.

12

GATLAND'S GRAND SLAM

BELIEF. IT'S just one little word, but for me it's the ingredient that enabled us to win the 2008 Grand Slam only a couple of months after Warren Gatland had taken charge. Belief gave us confidence, and confidence took our performance levels to a whole new level. We produced rugby during that year's Six Nations that many of us didn't believe we were capable of.

By the time we were due to play England in the opening game of the tournament, the new coaching trio of Warren Gatland, Shaun Edwards and Rob Howley had only been working with us a matter of a couple of weeks. And yet there was a whole new mindset amongst us as we set off for Twickenham. 'Hold on a minute. This England team simply isn't better than us' was the gist of our new outlook. You could sense that opinion trickling through the entire camp, and it was definitely the way I personally was beginning to feel. In fact, my thoughts were starting to go a step further – I actually thought that we were far better than them when I went through each individual player in every position. However, it took us until the second half of the game to decide to try and prove that what we were thinking was really the case. After we had gone out and done that, after we had indeed beaten England, all these feelings we had been having just started to magnify, and our confidence rocketed through the roof.

I believe that we have had the talent here in Wales for a number of years. You only have to look at the guys already in the squad and those pushing to get in to see that, but for reasons I cannot explain we haven't really recognised this or had the balls to go out and prove it.

The 2007–08 season saw Welsh rugby not only surge at Test level, but also at regional level as we started to punch our weight far more in EDF and Heineken Cup games. Just break it down for a moment. People have traditionally questioned the physicality of Wales's best players. Well, that's been reduced to rubble now. We are as physical as anyone. Our fitness was another area that was always scrutinised. With respect, that is a dead issue in relation to Wales players now. Just look at how strong we came on in the second half of each game during the Grand Slam. Then you have skills. I don't think I need to tell anyone that we more than hold our own on that front. Certainly, when I look at the England players, I consider our boys to be far more skilful.

It has just been the top six inches as far as we are concerned. Take someone such as Jonny Wilkinson. For so long, he was used to winning every time he pulled on an England jersey, and the same went for most of his teammates. They had evolved a winning habit – they didn't even contemplate defeat. We never had that. For years, we went into the Six Nations thinking, 'Ah well, it would be nice if we could come second or third this year.' England went in with one attitude only: 'We're playing for the Grand Slam. Nobody's going to beat us.'

Now I'm not suggesting that we become arrogant in the future, but that is the type of outlook we have to have in Wales. That's the outlook we had after we had beaten England, and I don't want to lose it. I'd rather that than the one we used to have, that's for sure.

Warren and Shaun have had a hell of a lot to do with instilling that mindset. I can recall playing for Wales and losing by 20, even 30 points, and then after the match looking at the opposition players and thinking, 'Our guys are better than theirs.' Or I'd look at my opposite number and think, 'I'm so much better a player than you are.' I could never understand it. But it took the 2008 Six Nations, and Warren and Shaun especially, to make me realise the importance of the top six inches.

As gutted as I felt for Gareth Jenkins when he departed, you couldn't fail as a player to be excited and perhaps a little wary about who would be brought in to replace him. Nigel Davies took command for the one-off Test against world champions South Africa in Cardiff in November 2007, but I wasn't involved because I had a niggling knee injury. With respect to Nigel, he was only keeping the seat warm for the new man, and he knew that. By then, after all manner of press speculation, we knew that the New Zealander Warren Gatland was that new man. He was the third Kiwi in ten years or so to get the nod, but I've always been of the opinion that nationality doesn't matter. It's all about the best man for the job, whether he's Welsh, Kiwi or any other nationality.

Whatever had happened with Gareth, I was impressed by the way the WRU went out to get the best man, and when it emerged that the new coach was to be Warren, there was an immediate buzz amongst the players, largely because of the success he had achieved with Wasps in his three years in the English Premiership. They were a team you couldn't fail to admire, particularly with Warren in charge. I liked the way they defended with their renowned blitz system – something I was used to at the Ospreys and hoped would be implemented with Wales – and was impressed by their whole approach to the game.

But Warren was just the first member of a pretty formidable double act – Shaun was soon appointed as well, and he was to have an almighty impact on us. The first thing I would say about him is that he is a person you instantly want to do well for, and when a coach can trigger that feeling among players, he has won half the battle. Shaun wasted no time in letting us know that he wasn't frightened to tell us if we weren't doing well. On top of that, he arrived as such a respected former player and coach that all the boys wanted to impress him, not just in matches, but on the training ground as well. I wanted Shaun to watch me train, see that I was working hard and then go back to Warren and say, 'Hey, I'm really pleased with the way Shane has approached everything. He's taken on board what I've asked him to do, and he's doing it really well.' It was obvious that I wasn't the only one thinking that way, because when Warren and Shaun arrived, the intensity of training increased hugely. It was like a bunch of school pupils trying to impress the headmaster.

The perception of Shaun as some sergeant major shouting and bawling incessantly is not a fair one. It does scant justice to the respect that Shaun affords all the boys. It's just that he will let you know if he is unhappy. During one of the first sessions with Warren and Shaun, we were doing a defensive drill. I had been used to hanging back for kicks, but Shaun spotted me dawdling and yelled at me to 'Get up on the fucking front line' in his best Wigan tones. You know what? The next time I made damn sure I was up on the front line. That's why he had yelled. Not for the sake of it or because he fancied having a pop, but to get the right reaction.

It was different from what we were used to, but it was the start of a culture that had us getting things right, no excuses. In the past, the approach had too often been to just hope that someone would learn from a mistake, the attitude being that perhaps they'd get it right next time. But the problem was that we didn't really learn often enough. Now the lads are on tenterhooks. The respect they have for the coaches means that they desperately want to get it right next time.

Most of us have had the hairdryer treatment. Mike Phillips in particular has had his fair share of rebukes, and he's not the type of fellow who takes well to being shouted at. But he respects the reasons why it is done, and just look at the improvement he made before his knee injury put him out of action just after the Six Nations.

With Warren and Shaun, it's like having two head coaches. However, Warren is by no means just an overseer. He gets stuck in on the training ground as well. Having been a hooker in his playing days, his focus is on the forwards, but he very much keeps tabs on everything we do. He chips in with what he feels we should be doing in defence and attack among the backs, even if he is prepared to leave the bulk of the work in those departments to Shaun and Rob.

Warren has struck me as a superb strategist. It's not a case of doing the same things in every game, because some teams play in different ways. Warren is good at working out a pattern that will get the better of a certain team if, say, they have a good lineout game or a good kicking back three. To be honest, it is a means of influencing the players' states of mind so that they believe the game plan is foolproof.

Rob is someone I hadn't worked with before, but he has impressed me a lot. They are a trio, really. There's very good chemistry between them, and the players see that and feed off it. One of the real triumphs has been the way they put together their sessions, which very rarely last more than an hour. Yet you get so much done in that hour. It's not just defence, it's attack, it's a minute drill – which basically means you batter into each other for a minute – and then you do a lineout or scrummaging session as well. And then that's it – you're done. The guys love it.

There's respect, and there's a bit of fear as well, which I think is healthy. Everyone knows that if they don't do things well, they won't be playing at the weekend. The key, though, is that there is no arrogance from the coaches. They do what they do for a reason, and there isn't a single Wales player who would say that they haven't seen the benefits in their own individual performances because of what the coaches do.

Warren and Shaun are open to suggestions, as other Wales coaches have been. They are not a dictatorship, and the boys know they can go and see them if they like. But I don't think anyone has had cause to do that yet. Players like to think they have got something out of a session if it has been tough, that is the difference. And current Wales sessions are tough. They will have even the fittest among us blowing out of our backsides. It's by no means just about getting a good head coach. It's about getting coaches in around him who know exactly what he wants and who complement his methods.

However, for all the improvement in our mental approach, I have to admit that I did not for a second think we would win the 2008 Grand Slam. The failure at the World Cup and the newness of Warren's regime were factors that I believed would play their part at some stage of the campaign. Yes, we felt we were going places, but not to the extent of winning a Grand Slam. And yet all those doubts evaporated after Twickenham when everything took on a whole new complexion.

We went into the England game knowing that we had been playing against these guys regularly for our regions and that it was high time we proved we could match them as a team when it really mattered. But come half-time it looked like it was going to be the same old story. To be frank, previous Wales sides that I have been involved in would have been ready to give up there and then. And we would have been completely out of it had Paul Sackey not been prevented from scoring by a fraction of a millimetre, because England would have gone in at the interval with a 23–6 lead.

I didn't feel the difference between the two teams at that point was down to anything specific. It was just that nobody was playing particularly well. I felt that all we needed to do was pull our fingers out. But at that stage I didn't know whether we were capable of doing so. Part of me was thinking, 'Here we go again.'

We had very little of the ball in the first half, and what we did have we wasted. England threw everything at us, and we were under real pressure. However, in the middle of that first period, I remember thinking, 'This lot aren't better than us.' I can always tell when a team is causing us significant problems and is really going to take some stopping.

The Sackey incident was our lifeline. I left the field frustrated at the halfway mark, but I genuinely believed we could turn it around – and 16–6 was hardly the most daunting of margins. I looked around at the England players as I walked down the tunnel and thought that they looked tired. They had given it a real go in the first forty minutes but had only scored one try. When I looked at our lads, it was the opposite – as if we had barely broken sweat.

Thankfully, by the time we got back to the changing-room, everyone, including the coaches, seemed to be thinking along the same lines. Shaun and Warren both got up and drummed the message home to us that we were still very much in the game. Shaun said that while he was disappointed to concede a try, he was impressed with the way we had defended. However, he thought we had to step it up even more.

Shaun addressed us as a group but also told a couple of boys individually what he felt they needed to do. I watched as the lads took his words in, and I gradually sensed that to a man we believed we could go back out and get the win. There was no beating of chests or head-butting doors. It was more of a quiet realisation, an almost telepathic understanding between the lads, that this was doable. The last words spoken were by one of the boys, I forget who, and they were just that we needed to start going through our patterns, keep the ball and let the result take care of itself. As I walked back out, I thought, 'I've been thinking exactly the same, so let's just get out there and do it.' And we did.

Our discipline had been shocking at the start of the game, but we started to go through some phases and get into the match far more. Our defence really tightened up as well. With every passing minute, you could feel the belief flooding back, and by the 50th minute I was saying to myself, 'We're going to beat these.'

Effort levels were at their maximum, and Mike Phillips's try, the one that would prove to be the winning score, epitomised our work ethic. Mike charged down a kick, helped secure the ball and then got on the end of the move to finish it off. It was an outstanding piece of play.

Gavin Henson really came into his own in the second period, too, having struggled to get into the match beforehand. When Lee Byrne got us back into it with his try, I think the hug he got from Gav was the biggest hit he took all day. That showed what it meant to Gav.

Maybe the best thing of all, though, was the manner in which we closed the win out – we were clinical. We kept hold of possession more or less on the English try line, rather than clinging on for dear life back in our own 22. That showed just how far we had come and how much we had grown throughout the game. I think if the match had lasted ten minutes longer, we would have ended up scoring one or two more tries and really rubbing their noses in it.

Winning felt sweet. All we had heard all week was that we hadn't won at Twickenham for 20 years and that Jonny Wilkinson was back and ready to shoot us down again. By the Friday, it was becoming a bit like a scratched record. Who knows, maybe some of us were starting to wonder if there was too much stacked against us. But I never picked up on that feeling.

We headed straight back to Cardiff that night, rather than staying in London, the main reason being that we only had a week's turnaround for the Scotland game. We spent the Saturday night at the Vale of Glamorgan Hotel, but we had a day off on the Sunday and went home to our families, which was nice and something I thought we all needed.

As wonderful as the win at Twickenham had been, we found ourselves coming home to the inevitable hysteria in Wales and all the dreaming about what we might go on to achieve. You can't blame the public for that. It's simply a result of what the game means in Wales, but with it comes mounting pressure, and the players were starting to feel it.

At the same time, things were starting to get easier. The longer we were together, the slicker we were becoming in training – and we had a very good week leading up to the clash with the Scots, who had lost badly to France at Murrayfield in their opening fixture. The standard of everything we were doing had gone up a level, and by the time match day arrived, confidence was soaring, and we were bouncing off the walls.

SHANE

All week, I had been having banter with Nikki Walker, the Scottish wing who is a teammate of mine at the Ospreys. Nikki's a great lad and a great player, too. I know because I have seen him at first hand in training. He's had a brilliant couple of seasons with the Ospreys, and I was on edge about playing against him, as you tend to be when you come up against somebody who is normally on your side. We both wished one another well, but we also both knew that the other one was desperate to come out on top in the game. We were playing a few mind games, but nothing major, because we get on well. I studied him all week on video, and I'm sure he did the same with me. By the time match day arrived, I thought I knew what I needed to do to nullify him.

And the best possible thing happened – I got an early try, which I know he wasn't happy about, and things just went from there. It was one of those games for me: I was busy all afternoon, got a lot of touches of the ball, which I always love, and seemed to be at the centre of all our attacking ploys. I even turned the ball over when tackling Nikki at one stage, which did wonders for my confidence.

Although I thought that we were always the superior side, Scotland kept in touch with us through the boot of Chris Paterson. Then, as the game was reaching the final quarter, I received the ball from close to a ruck, spotted a gap and went for it. I got past the first line of defence, and with the line and the corner flag looming I knew it was going to be close as Nikki lunged to try to stop me. I dotted the ball down and knew that it would go to the television official.

Was it a try? Yes, because it was given. No matter what people's opinions are on whether my foot was in touch, I will never say that it wasn't a try. I believe that it was, and I'm going to take every try and every point that comes my way.

Nikki, you might not be surprised to learn, thinks it should have been disallowed.

Sometimes you make your own luck in rugby. Sometimes if you have a go and back yourself, you get your reward. And when I get myself into those kinds of positions and I see the line beckoning, my determination to score is all-consuming. I just think to myself that there is no way I am going to make a mistake, spill the ball or allow myself to be tackled.

Those points were crucial ones for us, at an important stage of the championship, and I reckon that they were no more than we deserved. But maybe my second try against Scotland was further proof that the Grand Slam was meant to happen. On another day, that score would not have been given. We never looked back after it was awarded, running out 30–15 winners.

Next up were Italy at home, after a two-week break, and unsurprisingly most of the Welsh public by that stage expected us just to turn up and win. However, that is never the case against Italy, as our record in recent years shows. We've lost twice and drawn once with them since 2003, and we knew all about what a dogged side they were. They also had a new coach, the South African Nick Mallett, so were probably going through the same sort of rejuvenation that we were, with a fresh face bringing fresh ideas to the party.

I don't say this just for the sake of it. All the players knew that we could lose to the Italians, that they were a side who would revel in making life awkward for us. That said, our confidence was still high, and we knew that as long as we kept our wits about us we would probably come through, even if the Azzurri would take some wearing down.

It turned out to be very similar to the Scotland game. It was close at half-time, but we felt we were on top – and we went out and showed it in the second half. Our philosophy was to keep hold of the ball and that if we tested their defence enough times, it would open up. It did, several times, and we ended up running riot in a 47–8 win. In many ways, that result showed how far we had come. In the poor results against Italy in recent years, we had never been able to free ourselves from the shackles that they had placed on us early in the matches. We had always ended up frustrated, getting dragged down to their level. But this time it was different. We managed to impose ourselves and call the shots in terms of the pattern of the game, even though the early stages were a bit of a dogfight. Doing that is an art in itself in modern Test rugby. The difference in standard between teams is narrowing, and you have to bide your time in matches – you have to accept that you must earn the right to turn on the style. People said we softened the Italians up that day. Well, it wouldn't be my choice of words, but I can see their point.

Even now, there are those who contend that winning in Ireland was the game when the Grand Slam really became a possibility rather than just some distant dream. I wouldn't disagree. It was an absolutely thunderous win for us.

I was as nervous going into that Test as I had been for any match I have ever played in. It was a step into the unknown because of the way Ireland had played up to that point and because Croke Park would be a whole new experience for us.

The Irish had made a slow start, with an unconvincing 16–11 win at home to Italy, but even though they then lost to France in Paris, they looked like they were steadily improving and had scored some lovely tries in their previous game, a convincing win against the Scots. Because of these factors, we were afraid that this might be the game that they finally fired on all cylinders. Therefore, there was real apprehension in the squad. And quite apart from what they had done in the tournament up to that point, there was no doubting the quality of the Irish side and their consistency over recent years. They boasted so much experience, and they had walloped us on more than one occasion during the past few seasons.

There was so much at stake, and the fact that it was a blustery and unpredictable day weather-wise didn't help. I'm not one who gets overcome with nerves, but I was close that day. I'm glad nerves don't affect me to the extent they do others in the squad. Pictures of Neil Jenkins in his playing days vomiting during the anthems are well known, but he's not the only one. Our captain Ryan Jones suffers from the same reaction. He gets quite violently sick before matches. It's not pleasant. When one of the boys starts spewing, it sometimes triggers someone else off, and the smell can be overpowering. But you kind of get used to it, and if you can't handle foul smells, I wouldn't advise you to become a rugby player. I suppose everyone has their way of dealing with the pressure in the build-up to kick-off.

Routines tend to differ according to the time schedule. If it's a later kick-off, say 4 p.m., I will get up as early as I can, no later than 8 a.m., in order to have a decent breakfast and still be able to fit lunch in as well. I will have something light for breakfast, maybe cereal, a bit of toast and a cup of tea, but not anything like bacon and eggs. I have scoffed too much on a few occasions, and it does make me feel ill. Then it will be some pasta for lunch at about 1 p.m., or something else that is high in carbohydrates. You do have to time it right. If you don't, you can have a 'carb-rush' and find yourself going into a game with no energy and feeling really groggy. It's happened to me once or twice, and believe me it's the last thing you want. You feel on top of the world two hours before kick-off and then totally sapped of strength when it's time to take the field. I would say to anyone who plays rugby at any level that diet is important on the day of a game. It's something I wished I had paid more attention to when I first started playing, but back then nobody in Welsh rugby really knew enough about it.

There was an early kick-off that day in Dublin, and all I had to eat beforehand was a sort of brunch. It was probably a good thing that we started at 1.15 p.m. because my nerves would have kicked in to an even greater extent had it been later. I sensed a strange atmosphere on the way to the ground, even among the Welsh fans who had, yet again, travelled in their thousands. They are the most passionate and optimistic set of supporters, but I reckon a lot of them were also unsure as to whether we could clear this hurdle.

It turned out to be a real nail-biter – you didn't know which way the match was going to go until the very end. But that made the victory all the more special, and the way we closed it out, by clinically taking the ball into contact over and over again and retaining possession, the sort of thing the Irish prided themselves on, was so satisfying. It was yet another indication of the progress we had made. A few years before, we might have continued to try to run the ball all around the park. I'm not the kind of player who applauds the pick-and-go approach, for obvious reasons, but to see it executed so well by us was amazing.

It was certainly one of the toughest games I have ever been involved in. We were so up against it at half-time, with Mike Phillips in the sin-bin, but the resolution in the changing-room at the interval was once again to keep hold of the ball and let the gaps open up. I went to scrum-half as we kept it tight with Mike off the field, and I had a close-up view of just what effort the forwards put in during that period of the match. The success of the tactic to play controlled rugby really buoyed us. Slowly, we started to dominate the game.

We squandered a few overlaps before I managed to hand off Andrew Trimble and get over for the first try of the game. It was similar to the try against Scotland when I backed myself and went for it. There didn't seem to be a gap when I first received the ball, but a little dart put the Irish defenders off balance for a split second, and then I was fortunate that I got a good hand-off in on a player who is much bigger physically than me.

I'll say it again: the victory was a magnificent one. It showed that this team is capable of great things, although we have only demonstrated our potential in short spells up to now. I am convinced we can go on to become the best in the world. I really am. I think we were, on average, only producing our best for 40 or so minutes out of the 80 during the 2008 Grand Slam season, whereas the likes of New Zealand and South Africa invariably do it for at least 60. That's the only difference between us.

So, it was on to the final game against France, and for us to have come so far and not won that game would have been an absolute nightmare. But it was clear after the French team had been announced that it would be far from easy. Up to that point, their coach, Marc Lièvremont, had picked what looked like inexperienced and experimental sides and had come in for quite a bit of criticism for doing so. For our game, though, it was back to normal service, with most of their big hitters included.

The week in the run-up to the match was a long one. We trained hard, and there was loads of attention from the press and the public, with a lot of people turning up at the hotel wanting pictures and autographs. It was great to see people and very hard not to oblige each and every one of them. Some were coming down from north Wales, and to say no to them would have made me feel awful. But we didn't get five minutes' peace, and that was hard in a week in which we had to cover every angle in terms of match preparation. Although Ireland had been a tremendously difficult game, we were expecting the France one to be even harder.

There were moments when it was impossible not to stop and think about just how much was riding on the match. We wanted the Grand Slam so badly. We certainly weren't interested in not losing by 20 points and having the consolation of being tournament champions. To lift the trophy after losing to France would have been the most hollow victory.

I opened the curtains on the morning of the game, and the weather was miserable, so different from the brilliant sunshine that had greeted us on the final day of the 2005 Grand Slam. We knew the roof could be closed at the stadium so weren't too worried about how the conditions might affect the game, but I did wonder if the rain was some sort of omen. But when we got together before leaving the hotel, a couple of the boys said, 'Let's forget the weather and focus on ourselves.' It was a call I was more than happy to agree with.

We always gather together before getting on the bus and have a quick chat amongst ourselves. Warren also takes the opportunity to remind us of his expectations. However, the atmosphere was subdued that day. There were a lot of nervous faces, a lot of guys who were really twitchy. There are always nerves before every match, but this time it was different. Things were noticeably more tense. I got the impression that some of the lads were really worried about the way we were going to play.

I was as concerned as any of them. I knew I was going to come face to face with Vincent Clerc, who is not only one of the best wingers in the world, but who had been in sparkling form during the tournament, running in tries galore and proving himself a deadly finisher. I thought, 'If we are going to win today, I am going to have to play better than this guy.' I could see that the others were thinking the same. In such situations, you inevitably question whether you are ready as a team to take the next step and whether you are good enough as an individual to win your personal battle. I honestly felt that I was.

It was then time to make our way to the Millennium Stadium, and, as usual, we were roared out of the hotel reception by well-wishers as we headed for the bus. That's always a lovely moment, but that day it went over my head a little bit, because I was so wound up, the fear of losing worse than ever.

Nothing can prepare you for the sight that greets you as the team bus draws into Cardiff city centre on a match day, let alone Grand Slam Saturday. I can remember it taking my breath away when I played my first match for Wales, and it never fails to get my heart racing. There are days, like that one, when it seems all the more special. I couldn't get over it. I could see people shouting my name as I met their gaze out of the window, and all I could think of was how awful it would be to send them home disappointed, and that was before considering the millions watching at home or in pubs and clubs up and down the country.

Cardiff was a sea of red, but you could have heard a pin drop on the bus. Some of the boys close their eyes and listen to their iPods, others flick through a newspaper or a book, but I always look out of the window and take the sights in. St Mary's Street in the city centre that day was a real sight to behold. As we snaked along, I could see groups of boys spotting us and surging to the edge of the kerb to get the best view. A few individuals banged their encouragement on the side of the bus. To be honest, I find it very difficult not to get engrossed in the moment, even though you can cut the nervous tension with a knife. You feel like you are a gladiator being driven to the coliseum – though fortunately I've never encountered a lion at the stadium.

I love the whole business. I am still in awe of the situation, because I know what it is like to be on the other side of the fence. I have been to Cardiff with mates as a supporter to watch

Wales. I vividly remember going to watch the first game of the 1999 World Cup. Back then, I was one of the ones surging to get a view of the team bus.

When we arrived at the stadium, we went through the same routine we always followed. We got off the bus in our tracksuits and headed for the changing-room, where our kit was laid out for us. I always get a rush of excitement when I see the number 11 shirt dangling on a peg, and just above it there is always a brass plaque with your name and cap number engraved on it. Sometimes I read those two words, 'Shane Williams', and think, 'Wow, is that really me?' Maybe it doesn't have the same effect on others, but I am forever contemplating how I got myself into such a position and am thankful for the fact that I did. It gives me goosebumps.

At that stage of a match day, I am always nervous and a little fearful. I don't care what anyone says, all players at that point in proceedings are to some extent frightened of what lies in front of them. When you enter the changing-room at first it is quiet, but as the game gets closer it starts to get more rowdy. Some of the lads stay quiet right the way through to kick-off. I try to stay in my cubicle for as long as I can, just sitting and having some downtime. Others like to get changed straightaway and get out on the field, whether it's to do a bit of kicking or to warm up. Some, such as Alun Wyn Jones, like to wind themselves up as soon as they get there. He's like a spinning top: he's ready to go immediately. Ryan Jones will more than likely be in the shower throwing up. Martyn Williams will be walking around, chilled out, like he doesn't have a care in the world. It's a strange place to be. Despite how nervous I get, I will miss it when I stop playing.

When the match finally began, it followed a similar pattern to the previous encounters. The French put us under a huge amount of pressure, our discipline was poor at times and we really struggled to impose ourselves. But, again, our defence was watertight, and Shaun Edwards was happy about that at half-time.

At that stage it could have gone either way, but, just as at Twickenham, there was a massive determination among the boys during the interval to go out in the second half and get the game won. And that second half featured some of the best defence I have ever seen a Welsh side produce, which led to my try that broke the deadlock. France, under pressure in midfield, made a mess of a move, with their centre Yannick Jauzion overrunning a pass. The ball fell to ground, and I just managed to get my boot to it and kick it downfield.

There was no time to think. I put my foot down and hoped I would get there. I did, and, of course, it felt good, but I honestly didn't think about the fact that I had broken Gareth Thomas's Wales record of 40 tries when I got to the ball and grounded it. I was far more relieved just to have scored at a time when we desperately needed a try. The score really knocked the wind out of the French sails. It was a great time to get a try, and it gave us the momentum we needed to go on and win. Once again, brilliant defence allowed us to go on and get the victory, which spelled a night of bedlam in the Welsh capital and everywhere across the country. It was only a couple of minutes after I had scored that I thought about the record. The sense of relief that we had got our noses in front had been paramount.

What we had achieved took some time to sink in. Warren, rather than make a big speech in front of everyone, came around each of us individually to say what he wanted to say – that's the way he operates. He and Shaun congratulated all of us on our efforts, but we were all on cloud nine.

The magnitude of the achievement doesn't hit you at first. I can recall sitting in the dressing-room, exhausted and aching, looking around at the others and thinking, 'Have we really done this? Have we really won another Grand Slam?' I wondered if it would ever get better than that and thanked my lucky stars that I had been involved in not just one Grand Slam, but two.

The whole experience was like being caught up in a whirlwind. I got collared to do an interview by the side of the pitch immediately after the final whistle. I was speaking into the microphone when I saw the lads on their lap of honour out of the corner of my eye. I was so desperate to join them that I eventually had to break off from the interview and offer my apologies. I sprinted over to my teammates, and the feeling was just amazing. Almost the entire crowd stayed behind to join in the celebrations, and when you are walking around the pitch you can often hear what people are shouting at you. I could have kept walking around that field all week. I didn't want to leave the place. To me, it felt more special than 2005, because of the sheer effort we had put in and the way we had won the games.

Even after we had gone back to the changing-room and showered, there were still thousands of people left in the stadium when we came out for a photograph in our dinner suits an hour after the end. We headed over to the pub at the Brains brewery in the middle of town that night. There were drinks coming from everywhere as soon as the game finished. If it wasn't champagne, it was cans of lager. To be honest, it was impossible not to celebrate.

We ended up at the Oceana club in Cardiff, where they made the VIP area available, and after a few more there we left by a side entrance to get taxis back to the hotel – where hundreds of people were still celebrating at the bar. It was almost a never-ending evening, but it was nice at that stage to be able to chat to our wives, girlfriends and relatives. It was a good night and well organised, with us all together rather than in little groups off here, there and everywhere.

It was Sunday afternoon by the time I got home, but I had promised a friend of mine, Steve Phillips, who works for the WRU, that I would go to the Amman United clubhouse, because he had arranged to take the Triple Crown plate there. I wasn't in the best of states, with a bit of a hangover, but I was looking forward to seeing my friends and topping up with a few more beers. It turned out to be carnage.

I thought it would be quite low-key, but when I walked through the door, everyone stood up and clapped. Then the trophy was brought in. I tried to play it down, but it was clear what our achievements meant to everyone, and the recognition was wonderful. It was also nice for the local kids to be able to see the Triple Crown plate up close. It was quite a hard day in the end. I was all photographed out by about 6 p.m. and back home by 7 p.m., but what a time.

I should mention the supposed £25,000 my dad was reported to have won from a bet he placed on me to break the Welsh try record some years ago. I'm afraid I genuinely can't shed much light on it. I know that there was a bet of some sort, because my father had mentioned it to me and used to laugh and joke about it. But the first I heard of the £25,000 figure was when someone came up to me after the Grand Slam and said what had happened. It even made the front page of *The Sun* newspaper. I'm sorry, but he's been quite coy about it. Is it true? You'll have to ask him. It isn't really important to me, anyway.

If being part of a team that had won the Grand Slam wasn't good enough, I could also reflect on how well the 2008 Six Nations had gone for me personally. I was quite frustrated with the way I played against England. I didn't get the chances I would have liked, and with it being the first game under new coaches,

I really wanted to impress. But that made me determined to try harder in the later games, and luckily I got involved, gained confidence and got stronger and stronger. I got more and more attention as the tournament went on, largely because I was on the verge of breaking Gareth Thomas's try record.

Doing so meant everything to me. Being a winger in rugby is a bit like being a striker in football. You are there to score, and you know that if you do, your team will win more games than it loses. So, to have scored more tries than Alfie, Ieuan Evans, Phil Bennett and J.J. Williams is really something, as these are the players I have always watched and looked up to. To even be mentioned in the same sentence as them feels incredible.

But the try record did put me under more pressure during the campaign. People were asking me whether I felt I was playing my best-ever rugby, could I keep it going and could I go past Alfie's mark before the end of the championship. In a way, I am surprised by how well I dealt with it all.

In the end, things could not have gone any better for me, and there was one last piece of good news to come my way. Martyn Williams won the player of the tournament award after the 2005 championship, but I had forgotten about it, if truth be told. It wasn't something that was on my radar. Then one afternoon I received a call from the Ospreys asking me to go to Liberty Stadium to tie up a few loose ends. When I got there, the trophy was waiting for me, and the committee broke the news to me. I knew nothing of it beforehand, and it was a great surprise.

Actually, nobody would have complained had Martyn won it again, because he had had yet another outstanding championship, having decided to come out of retirement for the 2008 tournament. I was jumping with joy when Warren persuaded him to come back, simply because I knew that he was still one of the best opensides in the world. He certainly made my job easier, and to say he is one of the best in his position that Wales have ever had doesn't begin to do him justice.

As far as the backs are concerned, the number 7 is the most important player on the field, because he is the one who gets his hands dirty and puts his head in where it hurts to provide us with the ball. Not only that, though, you couldn't wish to meet a more grounded and modest fellow than Martyn, which makes his success on his return all the more deserved. Talk about a good decision to come back. But I guess it was my turn to take the overall award in 2008. And it sealed a truly unforgettable six weeks.

13

BEING AN OSPREY

IF MOVING from one club to another is a momentous enough change for a rugby player, then playing for a totally new outfit as part of a seismic step into the unknown is quite another. But that was the situation dozens of players in Wales found themselves in as the 2003–04 season was about to begin.

Welsh rugby had finally gone regional after years of debate over whether it was the way forward. Almost overnight, eleven clubs became five regions, and everyone was suddenly playing for different badges, even though Llanelli and Cardiff merely became the Blues and the Scarlets, as they dug their heels in and preserved their stand-alone status.

The doom mongers said that it would never work, particularly for the Neath–Swansea Ospreys – we have since just become the Ospreys – who were an amalgamation of two clubs who had traditionally been fierce rivals. Yet they were proved wrong. After five seasons as a regional entity, the Ospreys lead the way among the Welsh regions and have arguably embraced the provincial concept better than any of the others. For me, that's a source of pride, and playing for the badge actually means a hell of a lot to me these days. But it wasn't always like that.

When the news first broke about the regional revolution, I

was gutted, simply because I knew that it spelt the end of my days playing for Neath. I had enjoyed my time there so much, my mates were still there playing alongside me, I had a great rapport with the fans and the Gnoll had become a bit of a fortress. I didn't believe regional rugby would work. I didn't see how it could. I had never known Neath and Swansea to be anything other than bitter rivals, so how could we possibly function as a single entity? It was all wrong in my eyes and destined to flop.

The early days of the amalgamation were fraught and seemed to bear out my fears. At the outset, there was an awful lot of fuss between the two sets of fans over various issues, which made me wonder how we were ever going to get things moving. There were moans about the name, about the colour of the jersey and about where the majority of our matches should be played – the Gnoll or St Helen's. Some Neath fans didn't like the plans to play full-time at the Liberty Stadium, the ground we now share with Swansea City, because it was in Swansea. To be honest, I half expected the whole thing to be scrapped in a few weeks.

For weeks before the announcement about going regional, there were stories in the press about what was supposedly coming that made the players nervous, but when push came to shove it happened quickly. At first we were told what was happening by the club. They explained that some players would be offered deals under the new system and that others would not. That was tough to deal with, because I knew that some guys were effectively going to be out of a job – and so it turned out. Andy Moore, who was Neath's scrum-half at the time, had had a great couple of seasons, but because he was getting on in years he was discarded, which really disappointed me. Kevin James, the winger, was another one, and these guys were naturally disappointed.

I heard my fate after being called in to see Lyn Jones, and it was just a straight yes or no as to whether I was wanted by the Ospreys. I was then left to find out through Chinese whispers what fate had befallen the other boys. I remember walking in to see Lyn, and he simply said that there was a contract on the table for me to become an Osprey, and that was that. It was a relief, but nothing to get particularly excited about, because it had been such a turbulent few weeks.

It was at that time, during the closing stages of the 2002–03 season, that I had an offer to join Llanelli Scarlets – and let me tell you, I was very close to accepting it. The Scarlets represent my home patch at the end of the day, and Llanelli was the team I followed as a kid. I went to meet Gareth Jenkins, who was head coach at Stradey at the time, in an office in Llansamlet to discuss the move. Gareth said that he admired me as a player, that the Scarlets had been watching me for some time and that they really wanted me to come on board with them. They also offered me a good contract.

It was very tempting, and I thought long and hard about it. It was the first time in my career that I had received a firm offer to go and play somewhere else, and it did cross my mind that it might be time to seek pastures new and a fresh challenge in a different environment. I thought about it being the start of a new era and how a lot of other players were going to different places, wiping the slate clean and starting afresh, so why not me?

But something always drew me back to Neath and subsequently to the Ospreys. One factor was that a lot of the old Neath boys were staying with the Ospreys, guys I had grown up playing alongside, and I didn't want to part company with them lightly. And although the Ospreys were new, there would at least remain a strong Neath element to the team. I don't know why, but I also had a feeling that there was the potential for something very special to happen at the Ospreys – and I think I have since been proved right.

At the beginning, it was tremendously difficult for the two sets of players from different clubs who were used to playing the game differently and to different training methods. I was used to the ways of the Neath lads, and I suppose the Swansea boys probably felt the same about those who had been at St Helen's. I had played with some of the Swansea boys before, but culturally the two clubs were different. Of course, we were both Welsh and were only just down the road from each other, but in south Wales you don't need to travel far to encounter noticeable differences in approaches to sport and life itself.

In my opinion, Swansea at the time were more of a set-piece orientated team, who built their success around a dominant pack of forwards, whereas Neath under Lyn had developed a reputation for throwing it around a bit more. As a result, developing an Ospreys style of play did not happen overnight. It took a long time for us to blend. That led to many of the players questioning whether we had done the right thing, and it wasn't until the end of the first season that the majority of our squad started to have a bit more confidence in the new system and we finally began to get used to one another.

It was the same for the fans. Nowadays, they are brilliant. They have a fantastic stadium to watch us in, and they follow us in large numbers when we play important away matches. The way they have bought into what we have done has been outstanding, and I think the marketing people at the Ospreys should also take credit for that. But in the early days, I remember going to the nightclub Revolution in Swansea on one occasion to do a promotion for the Ospreys, and when we went on stage we were booed because we were wearing the black strip instead of the white one. There's none of that now – how times change.

As far as I was concerned, the most obvious benefit of the amalgamation was the chance to become a teammate of such great players as Scott Gibbs and Gavin Henson. Gavin particularly intrigued me. At the time, he was seen as somebody with enormous but as yet unfulfilled potential. He clearly had stacks of ability and offered something different. Working with him excited me, because I knew it would be different from anything I had encountered with other players.

By the end of our first season, I saw signs that we were settling down. This was demonstrated by the fact that we won the Celtic League the following year, which suggested that we were doing something right. We were helped by the demise of the Celtic Warriors, who were culled by the WRU after one year. This allowed us to bring in top players such as Sonny Parker and Ryan Jones, but by then we knew what we wanted to achieve, how we wanted to play and what we were all about, and everyone had got used to the players around them. There was a focus during the pre-season that had not been there previously and an acknowledgement that the teething problems had now largely been overcome.

Nobody was pleased to see the Warriors go under. It meant more fellow professionals out of work and was a huge blow for all those who had been involved with the only region that had no geographical reference in its name. The amalgamation between Bridgend and Pontypridd meant little to those teams' supporters, but they made big strides on the field in their first season, beating Wasps away in one Heineken Cup encounter, a fantastic achievement considering the English club went on to win the tournament that year. There's no getting away from the fact that the other regions profited from the Warriors' demise.

I think the one thing that has marked the Ospreys out from

their Welsh counterparts is the ambition and motivation we have shown in bringing players in, which is mostly down to the chairman, Mike Cuddy. He's been accused by some people of trying to hoover up every available player under the sun just to deny others the chance of signing them. That's rubbish. Mike wants one thing and one thing only: for the Ospreys to be one of the best teams in Europe. And he knows full well that achieving that in the modern era means going after the highest quality players.

It's not as though Mike buys players just for the sake of it. No, he helps fund signings in positions that we really need bolstering, and many of the new arrivals have had a galvanising effect on the squad. Just look at Filo Tiatia, a massive number 8 who is a daunting presence in the pack and whom so many of our guys feed off in matches. Ben Lewis, our young openside flanker, has benefited hugely from Filo's guidance, not to mention that of Marty Holah, our Kiwi flanker. The Ospreys' recruitment policy has been shrewd, and Justin Marshall at scrum-half was another example of a player whose arrival had a positive effect on not just the first team but the entire rugby operation, because of the knowledge, experience and guidance he had to offer after so many years at the top.

We now have two Celtic League titles to our name, having won what has since become the Magners League in 2006–07 with a late surge that held off our rivals the Cardiff Blues, who were also in contention in the closing couple of weeks of the season. We clinched that crown in an away game at Borders and were accused of not celebrating joyously enough, the suggestion being that it was a title that meant little to us behind the glittering prize of the Heineken Cup. But that was unfair. The somewhat muted reaction was more to do with the circumstances of the day.

It was the Borders' last ever game following the Scottish Rugby Union's decision to get rid of them for financial reasons, so there was quite a depressing atmosphere from the start. There was talk beforehand of there being a lot of emotion because it was the Borders' last hurrah, but it wasn't like that at all. I only sensed apathy among the home supporters, as if the match didn't matter, and that rubbed off on us in the end. The Ospreys fans who had travelled up to see us win tried to gee us up, and we did have a bit of a victory jig with a few bottles of bubbly flying about the place. But we knew before heading up there that if we won, it wasn't going to be a massive celebration. Sometimes, that's the way things work.

In my opinion, two titles in five years as a region isn't bad going. The Magners League has been decried by pundits and fans from the Celtic nations and England for not being competitive enough, the suspicion being that we don't give it enough respect and that it very much plays second fiddle to the Heineken Cup. I'll admit that Europe is the one we all want, but the Magners does matter to the players, and I sometimes think that the accusation that we don't care is exaggerated way too much. I know that I enjoy playing in the competition, and in my view the majority of matches are high quality and have a genuine intensity about them. The league is improving all the time.

The Irish sides have been criticised most for apparently paying the league lip service, but how do you square that with the fact that both Ulster and Leinster have won it? However, I will concede that Munster's approach has been slightly different. They are the one Irish side who place a massive emphasis on the Heineken Cup, and, well, that's up to them I suppose. Europe obviously means the world to them, to the extent that they are prepared to make sacrifices to their chances of winning the Magners. I'm certainly not going to argue that there is no difference between their Magners League team and their Heineken Cup team. But maybe they would argue that their record in the Heineken Cup justifies their approach.

The Scottish sides are also making strides. Edinburgh really took it to us to win at the Liberty at the end of last season. I can assure you that there was nothing half-hearted about that encounter.

All I can say is that I've enjoyed every season in the Celtic or Magners League. However, I wouldn't be against the introduction of play-offs at the end of the season to make the climax a bit more interesting. It has certainly worked in the Guinness Premiership, and maybe that would prolong the interest in the competition and jazz things up a bit for the supporters.

The Ospreys have certainly taken the Magners seriously, but it is hard to punch your weight on three fronts, which perhaps explains the Munster situation. What I mean is that I don't think it's any coincidence that last season when we won the EDF Energy Cup and had a real go at becoming the first Welsh team to win the Heineken, our Magners performances suffered to the point that we were never in contention to retain our crown and were playing for pride during the last couple of months. That wasn't acceptable to anyone involved with the region, and the fact that we failed to win a single away match the entire season was appalling for a team of our calibre.

Of course, the big attractions in the Magners League are the Welsh derbies. I can assure you that every time we face the Dragons, Blues or Scarlets, the intensity goes up a level, because it feels like there is much more riding on it. In particular, a fierce rivalry has developed between us and the Cardiff Blues, with some fairly barbed remarks passing between the two camps ahead of matches in the past. I've tried to stay out of that, but

I think if anything that the rivalry with the Blues stems from the fact that they too are a progressive region who want to be seen as the best in Wales, and, of course, they also have so many good players in their ranks. But, then again, Welsh pride dictates that there is a bit of needle between all four regions. There's always a lot of pride at stake, and the games sometimes feel like cup finals.

Individuals are invariably more keyed up because they are facing guys who are their rivals for a place in the Wales squad, and they want to prove a point to themselves and the national management. There are a few of the Wales lads who concern me whenever I play against them, whether it be because they are good defenders, attackers or whatever. Mark Jones, my Wales teammate who plays for the Scarlets, is a very good defender and is a handful in attack, someone you have to keep a constant eye on. Craig Morgan, the former Cardiff Blues wing, no longer plays in the Magners League, but he was someone who always used to cause problems. He was very quick and a dangerous attacker, and Richard Mustoe, who used to play for the Ospreys but is now at the Dragons, is another opponent whom I have a lot of respect for. Outside of Wales, Simon Webster is a very good operator for Edinburgh. He has a huge work rate and is very tricky to tackle and hard to defend against. Those sorts of guys can make you look lazy by getting themselves involved all over the pitch.

That is what I try to do. Whether or not I am directly involved in a move, I try to come in from all angles, to work around rucks and pop up here, there and everywhere. For me, the sign of a good winger is someone who could play anywhere in the backs if called upon.

There are times when I get the impression that the other Welsh teams are absolutely desperate to put one over on us because we are seen as the glamour boys, the expensively assembled squad, the Chelsea of Welsh rugby, if you like. It often feels as though everyone wants to be able to say they have beaten the Ospreys, and I can't help but laugh to myself about that, because all they are doing is playing into our hands by working themselves up. That kind of thing just motivates us even more.

A lot of teams come to the Liberty with the sole intention of stopping us play, rather than trying to dictate the pattern of the match themselves. It's flattering in a way, but it is also frustrating because it makes for a poor spectacle for the supporters. We played the Dragons at home towards the end of last season, and I swear that their team talk must have centred entirely on spoiling what we would try to do. Connacht are another outfit who are masters at that approach, but I think results suggest that it's a waste of time playing that way. If there's a lesson to be learned, it is surely in what Edinburgh did to us in May 2008. They were one of the few sides who came to us and tried to play – and they won.

In the summer of 2004, I was approached by the French club Castres to go out there and speak to them about signing. It was at the same time as Gareth Thomas was approached by Toulouse, where he ended up playing for three seasons. I was coming out of contract with the Ospreys, and I was very interested to begin with. I had played against Castres before, and they seemed like my kind of team. They had a slick, open, running style of play that I believed I could fit into well. I wasn't even sure where Castres was in France exactly, but the opportunity to go and experience something completely different excited me.

Gareth and I travelled out there together, because Castres and Toulouse were so close, and when we got there we both went our separate ways with representatives of each club. Bizarrely, though, we ran into each other in the same restaurant in Toulouse that night, each of us with the respective chairmen of the clubs, who seemed like they were the best of mates.

The trip went all right for me. Castres were offering me a sponsorship deal with L'Oréal, a car, a house and a very big salary. The whole package was a big annual earner, and I had to take that into account. I stayed in a hotel, but they took me to an area where there were properties within the price range they were allowing me, and I also met the coaches and players. Castres is a lovely little town, but it is quiet – nothing like Toulouse, which is a big, bustling city.

Gail and I were together at the time, and she accompanied me on the trip, but I don't think she was too keen on the move. I think she found the language and new way of life a bit intimidating. Castres seemed isolated, and I had never spoken French in my life – I did German at school.

Before travelling, I was extremely keen, but my enthusiasm waned once I'd been out there. The French hospitality was great, don't get me wrong, and the club gave me a huge welcome, but I was put off by how far away I would be from home, and when I came back, the Ospreys had got wind of the interest and had put together a new deal for me to stay with them.

Alfie told me he was going to sign for Toulouse, and I respected him for that. It took bravery and guts to make such an upheaval. But it wasn't for me. In the end, the homeboy in me came out, and that was that.

Alfie did really well out there and came back with a decent command of the language. He makes me wonder what such a move might have done for me as a person. But, then again, Castres is not Toulouse. Castres are a damn good club, a typically powerful French outfit, but Toulouse are giants and have a mystique about them that gives playing for them a whole new level of appeal. I knew that Alfie would be living in the city and wearing the jersey of a team that was seen as the Real Madrid of European rugby, and I felt a bit like I would be settling for the inferior, smaller club. But that was only a small part of it.

In the end, I told Castres that I wouldn't be joining them, and they were disappointed. It brought it home to me just how much they wanted me when they upped the offer a couple of times in a bid to get me to change my mind. They made no attempt to hide the fact that they were desperate for me to sign, telling me that I would be a definite first choice and would play as much as possible. It was never about those things, though. I appreciated what they did for me, and they were as good as gold, but, I repeat, it just wasn't for me.

I'm glad I stayed with the Ospreys. I've loved my time with them, and we have got to the stage now that we have built a brilliant squad that it is a pleasure to belong to and work with every day. Not only do we have great players, we have great characters, too.

A lot of people ask me about Gavin Henson. He's a guy who attracts more than his fair share of attention, and the fact that his partner is Charlotte Church only adds to the press and public's interest in him. Gav is certainly different, a unique sort of person. There seems to be a misconception among some people that he is full of himself and quite arrogant. Not true. He is quiet, he mostly keeps himself to himself and a lot of the attention he gets is unwarranted.

Rightly or wrongly, he seemed to acquire superstar status after playing a key part in Wales's 2005 Grand Slam. It was at that time that he met Charlotte, and media interest in them as a couple went through the roof. Gav's every move was monitored, and pictures of him started to crop up everywhere, even the most mundane shots of him getting out of his car to go shopping or leaving his front door. God help him if he ever stayed out late or went out in London. Photos of him would be plastered everywhere, and a lot of it turned into bad publicity. The slightest change in his hairdo would spark a feeding frenzy of scrutiny, and while Gav has freely admitted that he has enjoyed some aspects of the attention, it must also have been difficult to cope with. He has even appeared as a guest on *Friday Night with Jonathan Ross*, which I suppose says it all about his soaring profile. I actually think he does well to cope with the pressure, because although he can seem arrogant on the field – which stems from his supreme confidence in his own ability – he is fairly modest and reserved off it.

Gav does pride himself on his appearance. When he first came along, his fake tan, expensive hairdos and moisturisers caused a bit of a stir among the boys, because we all felt that those were the sorts of things that women go in for rather than men. Now, to some extent, we're all doing it. The majority of the Ospreys lads shave their legs these days, they really do, and Mike Phillips, Lee Byrne and James Hook aren't averse to sunbeds, either. I must confess that I've shaved my legs, the reason being the amount of strapping we wear. Trying to rip it off after matches can be painful, so it's easier to lose the hair.

However, if ever there's any criticism or scrutiny of this kind of thing, the first port of call is always Gav. But it's water off a duck's back to him. He is one of those guys who genuinely doesn't care what people think of him. Even when there's banter among the Ospreys boys, there's little point trying to take the piss out of Gav, because he's got the skin of a rhino.

James Hook is similar to Gav, in that he has tons of confidence when he's playing but is quiet off the field. James has taken fame in his stride. He hasn't been playing professional rugby for long, and already he's been put on a pedestal in Wales. James is a great guy, the sort who would do anything for anyone. The way he helped me when I had my testimonial was outstanding. Not only was he willing to play, but he also got involved in the publicity, which was a huge help.

Mike Phillips is a bit of a Jekyll and Hyde character, to be honest. On the field, he is one of the most arrogant and nasty players you will ever encounter. He's a very big and powerful lad, and he goes in for plenty of verbals. I played against him a lot when he was at the Scarlets and the Blues, and the number of times he has had me in a headlock is nobody's business. I definitely prefer him on my side.

Back in December 2005 – 22 December to be precise – we played the Blues at the Liberty Stadium, and I was getting married the next day. I was receiving texts from people such as Gethin Jenkins, trying to wind me up by saying that they were going to smash my face in for my wedding photos. At the kick-off, I tackled Mike, and as the play moved on he grabbed my head and rubbed it in the dirt, saying, 'Put that in your fucking wedding photos.' Afterwards, he said sorry, but there was really no need. 'It's OK, Mike,' I said to him. There was never the slightest bit of ill-feeling, and I laugh about it now.

When he's not playing, Mike is a gentleman and very down to earth, even if there is a bit of a mad streak in him. He is the type of player who likes to get in opponents' faces, and he never takes a backward step. That gives off the wrong impression to some fans, and I've had a few who've come up to me and said some fairly uncomplimentary things about him, but they don't know him as a person. Mike's one of the most passionate players I have played with or against. He's very aggressive on the field, but you need that.

In Mike and Justin Marshall – who left to join the French side

Montpellier in the summer of 2008 – the Ospreys probably had two of the best scrum-halves in the game and also two of the biggest characters. Justin certainly did not lack confidence, and why would he after what he has achieved? He is one of those guys who is always immaculately dressed. He never had a hair out of place, and he'd breeze around in his shades and expensive jackets and trousers. When he was with us, his social diary was always full, and he constantly had something on. If it wasn't a cricket day, it was a golf day; if it wasn't a golf day, it was a dinner or a charity function. That's the kind of guy he is. He's always busy and has fingers in many pies, like one of those suave city types.

Justin was always going to make his presence felt with us. When he first arrived, there was a story from his time at Leeds doing the rounds. Apparently, after they badly lost one game, Phil Davies, who was coach at Headingley at the time, brought the squad in the following morning for a tough session of sprints. The story went that the thrust of Phil's speech prior to the game had been about how they were all in this together, one for all, all for one, no matter how poor the season had been. Anyway, after doing a few sprints, the Leeds boys were standing in a line blowing hard but ready to go again when Justin said to Phil, 'Hey, if we're all in this together, why don't you get your arse on this line and do this with us?' Justin told us that was probably the end of his time at Leeds.

Because of stories such as that one, I found Justin a little bit intimidating when he first joined us, but for all his aura of self-confidence there was another side to him. He helped me enormously with my testimonial game, putting together an overseas side to play my Wales team and saying some very complimentary things about me to the media in the build-up. He didn't have to put himself out and go to so much trouble, and I won't forget that.

I was sorry to see him go, but that, unfortunately, is rugby. You get used to losing teammates and friends from year to year because of the way guys switch clubs.

Justin is coming to the end of his career, but I think Montpellier will suit him down to the ground. He will definitely have more opportunity to wear his shades in the south of France, and he'll get a better suntan. The French top-flight is fiercely demanding physically, but there's life in Justin yet, and I don't have the slightest doubt that he still has the class and skill to make a real impact there. At the end of the day, I think the Ospreys are a better squad from having had Justin Marshall in the ranks for a couple of seasons.

But the whole Ospreys squad mean a lot to me. I have played with Adam and Duncan Jones for most of my career. Along with Steve Tandy, we started out together as apprentices at Neath. Duncan is not just a teammate, but a mate full stop. We've been through so many ups and downs in the last ten years, and I feel lucky to have those three guys alongside me, whose games and characters I know inside out and whose company I feel totally comfortable in. They have always been there, whereas others have come and gone, and to have a constant like that in my career has been great.

Adam has had no end of criticism about his size and weight down the years. He would be the first person to admit that he has to train harder than others because of what nature has given him. But I wish his detractors could have seen how hard he has worked, season in, season out. I can assure you that, for his size, Adam is one of the fittest props you are likely to meet in rugby. His work rate and commitment are second to none. At Wales's conditioning camp in Wexford before the tour to South Africa in 2008, some of the physical demands put on the props were gruesome, and as hard as I was finding it I was just glad that I didn't play in the front row. On one occasion, I saw them in the gym pulling and pushing sleds with about 100 kilos of weight loaded on them, set after set. It looked horrific. Some of the boys were throwing up and nearly passing out, and as usual, Adam was giving it every last ounce of effort.

During the 2003 World Cup, Steve Hansen got into the habit of substituting Adam after 30 minutes. He had his reasons for that, but however Adam was feeling, it didn't really reflect well on him that he was being hauled off so soon in a game. I think it had a lot to do with him having been tagged as being unfit for so many years. But you cannot level that accusation at him now. I admire him for the way he has stuck at it and become an international-class tight-head who is not only very strong, but who can now still be going strong after 80 minutes of a tough Test match. He has a good shout to go on the Lions tour in 2009, and I would love to see him get selected.

On the loose-head side there's been a real tussle between Duncan Jones and Gethin Jenkins for supremacy and I'm just glad it's not me who has to decide between them. I know Duncan better from having been a club and regional teammate of his, and all I can say is that it is like having an extra back on the field at times when he is playing, such is the amount of ground he covers. But that's one of Gethin's strengths, too, and there is so little to choose between them. It's an example of the luxury of choice we have in certain positions in the Wales squad, with the other obvious one being the scrum-half berth, where Mike Phillips and Dwayne Peel are two of the best in the world.

All great sides need great cover in every position. Not many actually achieve that, but I think at the Ospreys we are fairly close. We're also fortunate to have Ryan Jones as our captain. When he first joined us following the break-up of the Warriors,

I didn't know much about him, because up to then he hadn't played much. But after one training session not long after he'd arrived, Lyn Jones came up to me and said, 'This Ryan Jones is something else. He's going to be great.'

That took me aback, because I had never really heard of him, but Lyn was right: Ryan is world class. As a captain, he is very thorough and works very closely with the coaches. For someone who has been at the top a relatively short time, he has superb leadership qualities and is one of those players who expects from you the kind of commitment that he himself gives, which is never less than the full quota.

And it's an approach that works, because the boys do play for him, which is the one key element all good captains must have. Ryan has become extremely influential in a short space of time and is one of the contenders to captain the Lions in South Africa in 2009. There are obviously other strong contenders, but in my opinion Ryan would do a great job.

The way I talk about our squad, you might wonder why we haven't won more in our short five-year history. Well, I can understand that, even though I maintain that two league titles and an EDF win is not to be sneezed at. Our victory against Leicester in the EDF final at Twickenham in April 2008 was particularly satisfying. The 23–6 scoreline was an indication of just how much we dominated one of the best teams in Europe.

We had learned a lot from what had happened to us against them in the same game the year before. In the 2007 final, we paid them too much respect and a dreadful first-half saw them establish a 28–9 lead, which effectively meant that the game was over. We threw off the shackles and rallied after the break. I managed to get two tries, but, in truth, we never really looked like winning it, and the final score of 41–35 was probably a touch flattering to us.

We were intimidated by their players, and I remember thinking during the match that we were shocking. I was frustrated that a guy such as Alesana Tuilagi, who was in direct opposition to me, was appearing to be a much better player. I knew he wasn't better than me – bigger, yes, but no way better. When you play against someone such as that who has such an obvious size advantage, the trick is to stay close to him. That way he can never build up a head of steam and run at you with any momentum. If you allow that to happen, it can be nigh on impossible to stop somebody of Tuilagi's stature. You just have to go in low and somehow try to bring him down.

During one Heineken Cup game against Sale, I found myself in just that situation. From a restart, the ball went to their giant French number 8, Sébastien Chabal, and he came hurtling at me. None of my teammates were near, so I knew that it was down to me to tackle him. As he got closer, all I could think was, 'Shit, I'm going to break a bone here.' I got him down and managed to stay in one piece, but it's not a situation I want to find myself in too often. Some players are monsters in the modern game, but you just have to put your body on the line and tackle them.

As far as the EDF was concerned, what a difference a year makes. When we faced Leicester in the 2008 final, they were not at the races, and we took full advantage, with tries from Andrew Bishop and Alun Wyn Jones handing us a deserved victory and our first ever cup success. James Hook was outstanding, proving that he can run games at the highest level. He slotted two conversions and three penalties, but it was his all-round game management that was most impressive. We had learned our lesson of not giving them too much respect, and this time we played with a confidence and belief that made our lives far easier.

But it is our failure to go further in the Heineken Cup last season that really sticks in the craw. We were genuinely fancied to go on and win the trophy and become the first Welsh club ever to do so. The Heineken Cup has become something of an obsession in Wales, because none of our teams has ever won it. I sense that there's a lot of annoyance about that.

Because of our squad strength, we were held up as real contenders, and rightly so. However, after Wales won the Grand Slam, expectation rocketed. Because so many of the same players were involved with the Ospreys, and with a potential semi-final in Cardiff and the final at the Millennium Stadium, people were understandably saying that we would never get a better chance to win it when we qualified for the last eight.

And we too believed we could do it. The pool stage had been a bit of a roller coaster, with us duelling with Gloucester for top spot in our group. But the Heineken Cup can be very unforgiving, with the ramifications of our opening-night defeat at Kingsholm ultimately proving costly. That was a match we let slip, much to our anger, although injury kept me from playing. Our performance was very good for the most part, but two vital errors led to tries against us. Again, I can remember watching it on TV at home and thinking that we paid them too much respect as we went down 26–18.

My theory was proved correct when Gloucester pitched up at the Liberty for the return clash in January. We thrashed them, and we did so with one of our best-ever performances in the competition. I got an early try, and our pack totally dominated, with Justin Marshall turning in a fantastic display behind them. It said it all about how frustrated they were that they picked up three yellow cards, and had it not been for a late consolation try by Ryan Lamb, the final score would have been even more damning for Gloucester.

It's easy to forget the maturity of our performance out in

Bourgoin in the final pool match that ensured our qualification in second place. That was a fine 28–21 success on French soil, where Welsh teams have notoriously struggled. But it wasn't enough to win us the pool, which meant that we had to travel for the quarter-final, playing Saracens at Vicarage Road, where we lost 19–10 in a game almost the entire population of Wales had expected us to win. That was because a fortnight earlier we had trounced the same side 30–3 at the Millennium Stadium in the EDF semi-finals, and the general consensus was that while Sarries would certainly make it harder for us in the Heineken game, they wouldn't have it in them to go the whole hog and put us out.

But that's exactly what they did, and it was one hell of a gut-wrencher. We had worked so hard to get to that stage and ended up letting ourselves down when it really counted. There were some defiant quotes from their players afterwards about how they felt that they had been written off and wanted to prove people wrong, but I don't believe it was a case of us being overconfident at all. It was just one of those days when we made a series of unforced and unexplained errors.

However, I do think there was a psychological factor at work, whether we realised it at the time or not. We had been harping on about the Heineken Cup all year, about its importance and how we had to do well in it, and I think that played on our minds that day. Our focus on the competition worked against us without us realising it.

The defeat was criminal. Saracens deserved it, no question about that, but I have no idea how we played so poorly with the quality of players we had on the pitch – it was mind-boggling. Afterwards, the scene in our dressing-room was horrible. We sat in stunned, bleary-eyed silence, with the rowdy celebrations from their camp audible from elsewhere in the stadium. But we didn't deserve anyone's sympathy. When you play professional rugby, defeat comes to everyone at some stage. A lot of us had just won a Grand Slam and things had been going so well, so perhaps we had taken a bit too much for granted. The defeat certainly brought us down to earth with a huge bump.

But we will come again in the Heineken Cup. I know we have said that before, but I really believe that we will have our day in the competition. We are too talented a squad not to. The Heineken Cup of 2008 was ours to lose – and we lost it. That's the way it goes. You are up against the best in Europe, and if we learned anything from the 2008 season, it was just how good you have to be to win that tournament.

Unfortunately, although we had no idea at the time, the defeat to Saracens seemed to contribute to Lyn Jones leaving us shortly afterwards. It was a development that came out of the blue for me. I received a phone call from Ryan Jones one afternoon in May asking me to a meeting with Andrew Hore. I couldn't get there, but an hour or so later Ryan phoned again to tell me that Lyn had left, as had fitness coach Huw Bevan. It knocked me for six, because Lyn was the only coach I had played for at club and regional level. He took a gamble on me as a young kid, and I will always feel as though I owe him a hell of a lot. I learned a huge amount from him. I was used to his ways; I knew how he worked and how to respond to him.

Plenty of people had been suggesting for a long while that it was time for Lyn to go, but I didn't share that view, and our failure to win the Heineken Cup was definitely not down to him. I don't know how many times I heard people say that Lyn had been at the club for long enough and that a change in direction was overdue. I think there is a school of thought that coaches have a shelf life – that unless they are winning trophies at the rate Sir Alex Ferguson does, there comes a time when the players need to hear a different voice that will energise them to greater heights.

I wouldn't dismiss that theory, because I have personal experience of it with Wales. Warren Gatland seemed to flick a switch with us when he arrived. No disrespect to Gareth Jenkins, but our whole approach changed, and perhaps there was a bit of a copycat element about the Ospreys' decision. That doesn't mean that I wanted to see Lyn go. But who knows? Perhaps he himself felt as though things had run their course and that it was time to seek pastures new. And whether we like it or not, we are professionals and have to move on.

One thing I do know is that it's been brilliant to have someone of Andrew Hore's calibre working for the Ospreys. Mike Cuddy told me at an early stage that they were determined to recruit him, and he now oversees the entire rugby operation. When he first arrived, he set about compiling loads of different reports as part of a wide-ranging review into how we do things. He is thorough and very passionate about what he does, so it can only be a good thing for the region. Our working relationship now is certainly different from the one we had at Wales, when I remember him shouting at me on the training field. Whatever role Horey plays, he is a person who gets things done, and his presence can only be a huge asset. From now on, we really have no excuse for not delivering more silverware.

14

A SPECIAL DAY

YOU ALWAYS appreciate the adulation you get from people when you have been successful, but there is something very special about having a testimonial, a game to pay tribute to your time with a particular club or perhaps your career as a whole. I was lucky enough to be granted a testimonial year by the Ospreys in 2008, and there were a whole host of events, including dinners and golf days, that will all provide great memories for me. I owe a massive debt of thanks to everyone who helped me organise everything. There were so many great events, but one very special moment was going back to my roots at Amman United with the Ospreys for a match that saw me play against my brother.

However, the undoubted highlight of my testimonial year was the match held at the Millennium Stadium on 17 May when I selected a Wales team to play against an overseas XV chosen by my ex-Ospreys teammate Justin Marshall. It was a day I will cherish for the rest of my life.

Both the Ospreys and the WRU were involved in setting it all up, with Steve Phillips, a friend of mine in the finance department of the WRU and an ex-teammate from my Amman United days, coming up with the original idea and doing a lot to make the day become reality. Steve took charge of the committee, while Justin and I tried our best to get as many players as we could to turn up, which was far from an easy task. In the professional era, there are so many demands on players' time, and the date we wanted them wasn't too convenient, because the English and French seasons hadn't finished. For example, we tried to get the All Black centre Aaron Mauger to play, but he had Guinness Premiership play-off commitments with Leicester to think about. Others had Heineken Cup and European Challenge Cup ties. We obviously wanted as many high-profile stars as we could get, but we were up against the schedules in the end, and there were quite a few players who just couldn't commit, for understandable reasons.

The week leading up to the game was one of the most stressful of my life. I was booking flights, cancelling flights, arranging hotels for players. There was just so much to do, and I wanted everything to be perfect. It was such a worry. I was afraid that next to nobody would turn up and that the whole day would be an embarrassing flop. Thankfully, those fears were not realised. The whole thing was wonderful.

The occasion got off to the perfect start when Georgie and I walked through a guard of honour onto the field. I think Georgie was cooler than I was – she loved it. She is one of those kids who cannot keep still at the best of times, and I thought she might be overwhelmed, but she was as cool as a cucumber, taking it all in her stride.

I spoke in the build-up to the game about it being an ideal way to brush off the cobwebs before the tour to South Africa, but nobody was pretending it was going to be a serious game. We wanted to make it meaningful, of course, but the emphasis was firmly on entertainment, and I think we delivered on that score, with well over a hundred points scored.

I enjoyed myself, but the final whistle in no way marked the end of the day. I did a few press interviews afterwards, and then went around all the boxes to meet the sponsors. By the time I had finished speaking to everyone, I had missed almost the entire FA Cup final between Cardiff City and Portsmouth, which was being played on TV screens at the stadium before the Konica Minolta Cup final between Pontypridd and my old club Neath, who much to my delight won the match. Not only that, but Gareth King, one of my mates, got the Man of the Match award.

I eventually hooked up with my family. Everyone was there, including my grandmother and grandfather and a whole host of aunties and uncles. To have everyone together meant the world to me. But there was one more group I had to meet – the three coach loads of supporters who had travelled from Amman United Rugby Club.

I received a phone call when I was with my family asking me to pop down to the St David's Suite, where they had been drinking all day: 'Are you coming down or what?' In the background, I could hear that it was carnage. I was dreading going into the room, knowing how drunk they were – and I wasn't disappointed. When I got to the door of the suite, the lady security guard turned to me and said, 'Are you sure you want to go in there?' I smiled and took the plunge.

It turned out to be quite an eye-opener. Again, everyone who counted was there: current mates, mates who I played with years ago, guys who I went to primary school with, people connected with the club in a variety of ways, and all the older guys and women who had supported me through thick and thin. But it was utter chaos. There were people rolling around on the floor, slipping everywhere. Some were sleeping off the effects of the booze already, and it was only 6 p.m. One guy saw me and ran over with a pen and paper only to go head over heels on his way. But it was brilliant to see them all. They had obviously had a great day, and the fact that they had made the effort to come meant the world.

Their bus left at about 6.30 p.m. Some went home to carry on the session, others stayed with me to continue the revelry in Cardiff, when it was my turn to have a couple of beers. We headed over to the Hilton Hotel, just across the road from Cardiff Castle, where all the players from both sides had gone to unwind. Well, it was the second time I was to walk in on a mass celebration, because they had been playing drinking games since the end of my match and weren't in much of a better state than the hordes from Amman.

They were having a ball, which was great to see. The entire bar was a sea of drinks, with about two glasses for every person, but I did have one concern niggling at the back of my mind – that the drinks were likely to be on my tab. I got a pleasant surprise when I went to the bar and ordered a beer, though. As I went to pay, the barmaid said not to worry, that Justin Marshall had put his credit card behind the bar and that it was all on him. 'Well, what a top bloke,' I thought and joined in with the fun.

We stayed at the Hilton for a while, and then we all headed over to Oceana, where they looked after us with bottles of champagne. Gail was with me, and by the end of the evening, we were both a bit worse for wear. When we went back to our room, six or seven of our friends were tucked up in our bed. We had to sleep on the floor. I kept waking up in the night wondering where I was.

The following Monday, we all went to the Ospreys' end-of-season dinner at the Liberty Stadium. It was a lovely evening, and before long I bumped into Justin. 'Great night on Saturday, mate,' he said. 'Really enjoyed myself.' We chatted for a few minutes, and just as I was about to move away he said, 'Hang on a minute, mate. I've got something for you.' He went off and came back with a piece of paper. It was a bill for the drinks at the Hilton: £1,450.

15

THE FUTURE

WE ALL need plans for the long-term. I have some, but I wouldn't say that they are exact at the moment. I think, to a certain extent, you just have to go with the flow, accept the hand fate deals you and make adjustments accordingly. Events change you. I know that now I am a husband and a father, I am different from the person I was three or four years ago, and I certainly have different priorities.

I wouldn't swap fatherhood for the world, and although we have a beautiful daughter in Georgie, I hope she will have a brother or sister in time. But Gail and I will never take anything for granted on that front again after discovering that life can take a cruel twist when you are least expecting it. In spring 2008, Gail fell pregnant, only to lose the baby. I know there are plenty of couples who go through this, but that doesn't make it any easier to deal with when it happens to you.

The pregnancy was planned. We both felt that Georgie was at an age that she would benefit from having a brother or sister, and when it happened, we were over the moon. Even though it was at a very early stage and you know there are things that can potentially go wrong, you still can't stop yourself thinking ahead. We both started to talk about names that we liked, and I said that it would be nice to have a boy who I could teach to play rugby. I also wondered what it would be like to have another girl and what she would like doing when she was older. That's how it goes. You simply don't expect the worst.

But when we went to the hospital for the first scan, we received horrible news. Gail knew what to expect, because she had been through it all before with Georgie, and when she saw the scan on the monitor, she looked at me and her face went red with anguish. She had seen that the baby had not formed, and even I could see that something wasn't right when I looked. The doctor told us that she couldn't find anything and that basically the baby hadn't formed. It was the kind of news that just rips you to pieces, and Gail got terribly upset.

We were immediately referred to a specialist at the hospital, and it was confirmed that the baby had not formed. We just had to accept that it was nature and be grateful that it had not happened later on in the pregnancy to a baby that had formed.

For a time, I couldn't stop thinking about it. It hit me hard, but I didn't want to get too upset in front of Gail, because it had already been tough enough on her. She's fine now, although it did knock her for six. However, the experience has not put us off adding to our family. I truly hope it happens for us when the time is right.

As far as playing goes, I have a real ambition to go on the British Lions tour to South Africa in the summer of 2009. Having been on the 2005 trip to New Zealand, I kind of feel that I have a bit of unfinished business in that particular jersey. It's exciting to anticipate what a really strong British and Irish team could do down there, and I think if they get it right in terms of the size of the squad and all the other trimmings that go with it, the Lions could be successful.

I know one thing: after the whitewash in New Zealand in 2005, the Lions need to be successful this time for the sake of their future. I believe that in appointing someone of the stature of Ian McGeechan as head coach, they have given themselves every chance of doing that. I know that if I want to be involved, I have to play a lot of good rugby leading up to the tour, because I hope that the squad will be selected on current form rather than on reputation.

I remember the last Lions tour to South Africa as being one of the best I have ever seen. They toured as the underdogs against the Boks, who were world champions then like they will be in 2009. The Lions spent a lot of time on the back foot, but the way the series was clinched with a Jeremy Guscott drop goal was memorable. And I can't help but recall the contributions of Neil Jenkins and Scott Gibbs – Neil with his dead-eyed kicking and Scott with, among other things, that infamous charge on the prop Os du Randt. How amazing it would be to be involved in a repeat of something like that.

But having just returned from that country, I know just how demanding it will be. However, that just makes the potential reward all the more tantalising. McGeechan visited the Wales camp in South Africa in 2008, getting his bearings and probably making early plans for 2009. I think we can be sure that he will leave nothing to chance. If the Lions don't pull it off, it will not be for the want of doing their homework.

As for the Ospreys, I have three years left on my contract, including the 2008–09 season. I expect to see that out and then maybe stop playing altogether at a time when I will hopefully have achieved everything I could have wanted to. As I said in earlier chapters, while I feel privileged to be a professional sportsman, I have always played rugby – and anything else, for that matter – for the love of it. I still like going down the local park for a kickabout with my mates and my brother. I'd like to play for the local sides when I stop playing professionally, even football. When I started playing, it was for the social aspect, and that is the reason I ended up where I did. I was always relaxed, I played with a smile on my face and I was confident in my ability. I played my best because of that attitude and got myself noticed. Even when I pop down to watch the Amman now, I am itching to get on the field and play. I'd love to go back to that at the end of my career, playing for a couple of pints – maybe more if we win – and just doing it for the hell of it.

I am lucky in terms of my physical fitness. Most people would consider my age (32 when this book went to print) to be the wrong side of the hill in terms of a man's physical peak. However, I played probably the best rugby of my life in 2008. The subject was brought up quite a bit by journalists, and all I could say was that I felt stronger, fitter and faster than ever. And I believe actions spoke louder than words on that front.

It doesn't just happen, though. There is a price to pay. I have always trained hard, but these days I pay more attention than ever to looking after my body, eating the right things and doing extra fitness work on top of what my coaches tell me to do. The best thing is that I feel good within myself. You can't ask for much more than that.

Saying all that, nobody needs to tell me that the position I play does not suit the older generation, unlike props, second rows and flankers, who can go on until they are 36 or so. That is why I can see myself hanging up my boots in three years' time – I do not expect to have the speed then that I do now. I might surprise myself. I might turn out to be a bit of a freak of nature, and if that is the case, I will go on. But I really can't see that happening. I think I will know straightaway when I have lost that vital yard of pace or the ability to sidestep like

I know I can. Let me tell you, I'm not looking forward to that day, because I love being quick. I love being able to get the ball in my hands and I love beating players. That's why I play the game. The day it all leaves me, I will be gutted, but, unfortunately, we all get old.

To be honest, I think it was great of the Ospreys to show faith in me by giving me a three-year deal when I was thirty-two. I asked for talks during the Six Nations when things were going so well and I realised that I only had one year left on my old deal. At first, I was thinking about a two-year contract, but then I decided to push for three, and they agreed. I don't think they need worry. I think that I have a good three years still left in the tank, but I suppose only time will tell. Rugby is a funny old game.

In terms of international rugby, I plan to be the one who decides when I quit, not someone else. The attitude of some players – Gareth Thomas and Allan Bateman being two – is never to retire. They go on making themselves available as long as they are playing and wait until they are not selected. I won't do that. I will know when it is time to leave the Test scene. I do not ever want to be on a field for Wales knowing that my opposite number is better than me and that there is nothing I can do about it because the powers I once had are on the wane. The last thing I want to happen is to be made a fool of. I never want to be picked for the sake of it, and I will know when I don't deserve to be selected any more.

While I have spoken about playing for fun at the end of my professional days, I also know that I am going to need a life outside of rugby, and, of course, a means of earning a living. I think I will be strengthening my property portfolio in the next few years, and I am hoping to be able to fall back on that to some extent. At the moment, including plots of land, I own about ten properties. At first I bought them more as a hobby, but now it is more of a proper business.

I have also been approached to do TV work by a couple of companies, although there is nothing on the table as yet. That is something I will definitely look at, although I don't know if I can see myself doing it full-time. I suppose I have an advantage in that I can speak Welsh, but I'll see what develops. I do enjoy media work, though, and I like doing some of the more light-hearted stuff, rather than just talking serious rugby all the time.

In terms of the property side of things, I am putting a few things in place that will hopefully give me a regular income when the monthly cheques from the Ospreys are no longer coming in. I also have the option to work with the Ospreys when my contract finishes. Precisely what that would entail, I don't know – whether it would be in a coaching capacity or something on the commercial or junior-development side. Who knows what the situation will be down the line?

I doubt I will end up in senior coaching. I wouldn't totally rule it out, but from what I have seen in the modern game, it is a pretty ruthless profession, and I don't know if my stress levels could cope with it. The most important thing is to have options and to start putting things in place, rather than finishing playing and then starting to worry about it.

16

MY ALL-TIME TEAM

ONE OF the hardest things I have ever had to do was pick my own Wales team for my testimonial match. Throughout my career, I have been the one selected, so it was a situation that was totally alien.

When Warren Gatland agreed to coach my team for the day, I naturally assumed that he would be the one making the decisions, but he thrust that responsibility on my shoulders, and let's just say it's one that I could have done without. As it turned out, the friendly nature of the match meant that there was a glut of substitutions, so the players didn't take anything to heart – or at least I hope they didn't. But it was inevitable that the team I chose to start the game would be interpreted as my first-choice XV. Choosing between James Hook and Stephen Jones, Gethin Jenkins and Duncan Jones, etc., is not something I would want to do on a regular basis. Perhaps that's why coaching doesn't appeal to me too much at the moment.

Still, the challenge of picking an all-time XV of players I have played alongside was too tempting to pass up. Again, it has been far from easy, and in six months' time I could feel differently about some of the positions. Those I have not singled out will get over it, I am sure. Suffice to say, there are dozens of players who have my utmost respect – way too many to be included in one team. Anyway, here goes:

15. JASON ROBINSON

Jason was one of those players who I think got better with age, and when he decided to retire after the 2007 World Cup, it was a major loss to England. There have been few players like him. He was one of the most devastating counter-attackers the game has ever seen, and his ability to step off either foot at blistering speed took your breath away at times. Jason was one of the best examples of a guy who made switching codes look easy. Not only that, but he is a hell of a nice guy. We got on very well on the Lions tour to New Zealand in 2005.

14. GARETH THOMAS

Alfie could play several positions, but I'm placing him on the wing. You just cannot argue with what the guy has achieved in his career. I don't care what anyone says, to clock up 100 caps is something to be extremely proud of. Alfie had it all: skill, pace and a fearless approach. He led Wales with a passion, having been a figure many people didn't believe could do the job. A legend of the Welsh game.

13. ALLAN BATEMAN

I used to love playing alongside him at Neath. He was so good, he made life easier for me on the wing. His defence was outstanding. I can barely recall him ever being outfoxed one-on-one by an attacker. And then, of course, there was his fitness, which was well known and admired throughout the game and the reason why he was able to play at such a high level for so long. It was to the loss of the union game in Wales that he spent some of his best years in league.

12. GAVIN HENSON

Gav's had his ups and downs throughout his career, but the fact is that he is world class. It's not only great to play alongside someone like him, but to train with him, too. He is simply one of the most outrageous talents I have ever encountered. Gav is skilful, he is brave and strong, he has a right boot to die for, but perhaps above all it is his sheer game awareness that stands out. He sees things before others do, and that buys him and his teammates precious time in match situations.

11. MARK JONES

Mark is one of the most graceful runners in the game. He has blistering pace when he gets into full flight, and his defence is underestimated. He'll stick his head in where it hurts against far bigger men. But one of the things I most admire about him is his strength of character. To come back from not just one but two horrendous knee injuries in the way he has is nothing short of superhuman – and he hasn't lost an ounce of his old pace in the process. It is a phenomenal achievement. I far prefer playing with him for Wales than against him when the Ospreys play the Scarlets.

10. NEIL JENKINS (JAMES HOOK)

This was the toughest choice to make, and I very nearly copped out and picked both of them – they could play a half each if we ever get this team out onto a pitch. I have played with some great number 10s in my time. Neil Jenkins had so much to offer and was obviously one of the best kickers there has ever been, but I think James Hook will be a better player than he is now in a few years time and up there with the likes of Jinks. Jinks is a great guy who came through some tough times with Wales to be one of the truly legendary outside-halves. I just could not split these two for ages, although because of what he has already done I gave it to Jinks on the understanding that Hooky will go on to become a legend. And I can't move away from this position without saluting Stephen Jones, who I have played so much rugby with and who I think is a great player and person.

9. ROB HOWLEY

Another toughie, but Rob Howley gets the nod. I was fortunate enough to play alongside Rob for Wales at a time when he was almost certainly the best in his position in the world. He had a brilliant attitude to preparation, his passing was pinpoint, and his pace and energy singled him out from the rest. Rob was another who could spot things before others, and it was very often too late before opposition defences knew what he was up to. But Wales are lucky at the moment to have three scrum-halves such as Gareth Cooper, Mike Phillips and Dwayne Peel. I think we're spoilt for choice in that department.

1. DUNCAN JONES

There are loads of great loose-head props around the world, I know, but I have worked with Duncan for more than a decade so know him better than most. We started our professional rugby together at Neath and are great friends. That means I have seen at close quarters over a long period of time what he brings to a team. Duncan is dynamic, a hugely talented and skilful footballer for his position, and I have never known him take a backward step against anybody.

2. MEFIN DAVIES

I'm not pretending the front row is a department I know a huge amount about, but I do know that I have played with some great hookers, including Garin Jenkins and Robin McBryde. But the fellow who gets my vote for this position is Mefin Davies. I've played alongside him for Neath and Wales, and he was at the Gnoll when I first arrived. Mefin is such a gritty player. It took him a while to get his Wales caps, but when they did arrive, they were well deserved. I have to say, though, that Huw Bennett at the Ospreys is a player who has improved massively in recent years.

3. ADAM JONES

Again, front-row play is a bit like Japanese to me, but I am going for Adam on the basis that, like Duncan, I have seen him at close quarters season after season. I know the hard work he has put into becoming a respected prop on the world stage and the dedication he has put into reaching top physical condition. Adam has been a towering presence in the Ospreys and Wales scrum.

4. CHRIS WYATT

There will be wry smiles on the faces of some people at this selection, but Graham Henry once summed Chris up by saying that he was one of the best second rows in the world. On his day, that was most definitely what he was. Chris had size, was one of the best lineout jumpers of his generation, and in his pomp he also had an athleticism that his opponents envied. Chris was a character and didn't flourish as some predicted he would, for reasons he is best placed to explain, but I will always admire him.

5. PAUL O'CONNELL

I stress that my Ospreys and Wales colleagues Alun Wyn Jones and Ian Evans are going to be world class long after I have hung up my boots, but having been on a Lions tour I would have to include the Irishman. He is not so well respected for nothing. He has a wide range of skills but is also a tremendous ball-carrier and very aggressive on the field, with a fierce will to win. Before anything else, though, he is just a huge man, the type who you don't ever want to have running at you at any kind of pace. O'Connell is worth his weight in gold.

6. RICHARD HILL

Simply one of the best back-row forwards there has ever been. When I saw him at close quarters on the Lions tour of 2005, he was probably past his very best. However, you couldn't fail to bow to his dedication, professionalism and will to win. Sir Clive Woodward singled him out as the best he has ever worked with, and that doesn't surprise me at all. Hill, by his sheer presence alone, was instrumental in our defeat by Saracens in the Heineken Cup in 2008.

7. MARTYN WILLIAMS

It was very difficult to pick this position, because I have played with so many great opensides. Marty Holah at the Ospreys is probably the rock of our pack. He does so many things well and seems to be everywhere at times, winning a huge amount of ball at the breakdown. Brett Sinkinson at Neath was imperious before he got caught up in the Grannygate saga and was one of the best tackle-jacklers (tackling and winning the ball) I have ever seen. But Martyn Williams gets it. I have played against him for the Ospreys and alongside him for Wales so know just what a menace he is. A great player, he always backs himself in any situation and his work rate is phenomenal. He is a true gentleman as well.

8. SCOTT QUINNELL

I don't wish to labour the point, but this is yet another berth that is tough to choose. For starters, there is Lawrence Dallaglio, who I worked alongside on the Lions tour. He is one of the best number 8s ever to have played the game, but having barely played alongside him, I'm ruling him out. Then there's Ryan Jones, already one of the best back-rowers in the world and a great captain. Ryan, like some I have already mentioned, is destined for even bigger things and will only get better and better as time goes on. I expect 2009 to be a huge year for him. Another player whom I have enormous regard for is my Ospreys colleague Filo Tiatia. He is such a strong and powerful customer, and a great rugby player who always delivers a performance. But, for me, it has to be Scott Quinnell. When I started playing for Wales, he was arguably the best in the world in his position, and he edges it ahead of Filo. His power, skills and ball-carrying ability were unrivalled for a time, and he was the heartbeat of the Wales and Scarlets teams. A true great.

COACHES: WARREN GATLAND AND SHAUN EDWARDS

I'd be in trouble if I picked anyone else. But, seriously, I have chosen them for no other reason than that in the short time I have worked with them, I have learned so much and improved dramatically as a player. They have so much to offer. They come as a package, and the reason for that is that they work so well together.

I have worked with some great coaches for Wales, all of whom have had superb qualities. I rated Steve Hansen very highly, even though he didn't pick me for most of his reign. I had loads of time for Graham Henry – probably because he was the first to give me a chance with Wales. Graham had a marvellous rugby brain, and his track record speaks for itself. I have to mention

Lyn Jones as well. We became friends as well as colleagues, and, as I mentioned earlier, although Lyn is a bit of a one-off, he knows the game and has much to offer.

17

QUESTIONS, QUESTIONS

What advice would you give to young players?

Don't take rugby too seriously. Try to play it with a smile on your face. One of the dangers for young players these days is that they become obsessed with rugby, that it dominates their every waking thought. There is nothing wrong with being dedicated, and I would say to any aspiring player that without hard work you won't get anywhere, but there is a difference between that and letting the sport take over your life. If you take it to the extreme that rugby is the first thing you think of when you wake up and the last when you go to bed at night, then it becomes unhealthy, in my view. That is when youngsters start to feel pressured into trying to become something that is possibly out of their reach.

I have always found that by enjoying the game and playing with a smile on my face, I produce my best. If you do that and you have the ability, you will come through with a reasonable level of hard work. I go home after training or a game and try to switch off from rugby. It cannot be your life 24 hours a day. If that happens, it will no longer be any fun. I still enjoy my rugby now, and I hope I always will. I analyse, I work hard in training and I sometimes do extra, but, at the end of the day, I am able to forget about rugby, too. Do your work, play hard, be competitive, do the simple things right and if it is meant to be, it will happen.

What is your most embarrassing moment?

I can't think of a time when I have been more embarrassed than when I made the mistake that gave Émile N'Tamack a run-in for a try on my first Wales appearance. You have to remember that I was the new boy at the time, and to make that kind of howler in front of so many of your countrymen, who were probably thinking, 'Who the hell is this bloke?', took a bit of getting over. I was made fun of by the boys for years after that.

What do you like to watch on television?

I've always been a huge fan of *The Simpsons*. I like the unreality of it all, and the programme reflects my personality, in that I don't take life too seriously. If I could live in a cartoon world, I probably would, especially Springfield. You know, in many respects, I'm not all that dissimilar to Homer Simpson.

What music do you like?

I grew up in the 1990s with the likes of N-Trance and the disco tunes of Haddaway and the Urban Cookie Collective. But nowadays there isn't really a style of music that I strongly dislike. I listen to the Foo Fighters a lot, but anything else that comes along is fine, too. I like almost every sort of music, even classical at times. I especially like the soundtracks to the films *Platoon* and *Gladiator*. But if you put it in the CD player, I'll listen to it and give it a chance, whether it's R & B, dance or classical.

What annoys you in life?

I hate liars, blatant liars. Whether it's a little white lie or a real howler, it's a trait that really annoys me. I also can't stand tight people; for example, people who lend you a fiver and then want it back the next day without fail, or someone you gave a tenner to a year ago who then asks you for the money if he goes and buys a newspaper for you. Little things like that niggle away at me – and they have happened to me plenty of times in the past.

Playing rugby in strong winds destroys me.

Who from other sports do you most admire?

Tiger Woods. Golf is not a game I have played a huge amount of in the past, but I have got slightly more into it in recent times. Having done so, I know just how difficult a sport it is to master. So, to see someone such as Woods make it look so easy and beat the best in the world over the toughest courses on such a consistent basis is just breathtaking. His win at the US Open in 2008 when he was virtually on one leg because of a knee injury was just fantastic. He has 14 major championships in his locker. I will be staggered if he doesn't finish with more than the 18 Jack Nicklaus bagged. Don't tell me Tiger Woods isn't the best sportsman who has ever lived.

What is your favourite meal?

Christmas dinner. When I was a kid, with my parents being divorced, I used to have three Christmas dinners – one with my mam, one with my dad and one at my gran's. I used to enjoy them all. I love the turkey and stuffing, although I'm actually not keen on vegetables, other than raw carrot.

What's your all-time favourite film/actor/actress?

I'm a big Jim Carey fan, and *Ace Ventura: Pet Detective* wins my vote. It doesn't matter what film Jim Carey is in, I will watch it. I just think he is so funny and talented. I think he's the type of actor you either love or hate, and I do know a lot of people who fall into the latter category. I was overjoyed when a sequel to *Ace Ventura* was brought out. Like the first one, it was slated in the press, but I didn't care – I loved it.

As a kid, I idolised Doris Day and used to watch all her films. I can't really give a reason why, and when me and my gran speak about it now, she can't believe it.

What's been your worst celebration hangover?

As alluded to earlier, it was after the Grand Slam win in 2005. I started on the lager and graduated to sambuca, downing about 20 glasses of the stuff. I was carried out of the place. The next morning, I was sick everywhere, my head was banging and I knew I had to drink again all day. Fortunately, the hair of the dog worked that day, and it was worth it in the end.

Where were you most surprised to be recognised?

When I went on Wales's summer tour to Japan in 2001, it was still not all that long since I had begun playing Test rugby. One evening when we were strolling down the street, I was recognised by a group of people. I was flabbergasted, and I guess it just goes to show how much interest there is in rugby in Japan.

What's the hardest tackle you've ever taken on a rugby field?

I was tackled by Bakkies Botha when South Africa came to Cardiff to play us in the autumn of 2004. I had just sidestepped their loose-head prop and was running straight when he came from nowhere and smashed into me from the side. I was completely winded, and to make matters worse the ball was dislodged and they scored at the other end of the field. I had been playing an American Football computer game incessantly in the build-up to that game, and after Botha hit me, I swear for 20 minutes I thought I was in that game. I couldn't tell the difference between real life and the game. That was how hard he hit me – right into a computer game. After the match, I didn't have a clue where I was for a spell. It was one of the strangest experiences I have ever had.

What is the most disappointed you have been after a game?

We played New Zealand in the autumn of 2005 after winning the Grand Slam, and naturally it was a period when much was expected of us. A bit like in South Africa in the summer of 2008, we were looking to take the next step against the southern-hemisphere superpowers, having been crowned European champions. But we were thrashed 41–3, and to make matters worse my opposite number, Ricoh Gear, scored a hat-trick. On a personal level, he got the better of me by some margin. I was totally gutted. The only other time to compare was losing to Fiji at the last World Cup – and I think I've said enough about that.

What would you change in rugby?

None of the rules, because I don't know most of them anyway. What can I say? Perhaps I would bring in size and weight restrictions to make me look a better player.

Appendix

CAREER STATISTICS

NEATH

YEAR	APPEARANCES	TRIES	CONVERSIONS	PENALTIES
1997–98	10 (+1 as a sub)	1		
1998–99	23 (+3)	15	1	
1999–2000	28	17		
2000–01	30	15	39	59
2001–02	2 (+1)	3		
2002–03	30 (+1)	20		
Total	123 (+6)	71	40	59

Shane's Neath debut was as a replacement versus Pembroke County on 17 March 1998. He scored a try from scrum-half, and Neath won 48–15. His league debut came the following season as a replacement versus Aberavon at the Talbot Athletic Ground. Neath won 37–27. The Neath team that day was: Geraint Evans; Dave Tiueti, John Colderly, Tristan Davies, Ian Jones; Luke Richards, Stefan Jenkins (Shane Williams); Duncan Jones, Mefin Davies (captain), Mike Morgan (Leighton Gerrard); Steve Martin (Mike Turner), Adam Jackson; Richard Francis, Scott Eggar, Brett Sinkinson.

OSPREYS

2003

DATE	OPPONENTS	SCORE	TRIES
29 Nov	Leinster	25–36	
7 Dec	Leeds Carnegie	20–29	1
12 Dec	Edinburgh	16–32	

2004

DATE	OPPONENTS	SCORE	TRIES
2 Jan	Llanelli Scarlets	15–28	
10 Jan	Stade Toulousain	6–29	
16 Jan	Stade Toulousain	15–28	
23 Jan	Edinburgh	15–33	
31 Jan	Leeds Carnegie	10–3	
3 Apr	Connacht	21–24	
16 Apr	Border Reivers	60–7	2
30 Apr	Leinster	16–16	1
9 May	Llanelli Scarlets	15–18	1
14 May	Glasgow Warriors	31–34	
3 Sept	Munster	34–17	
10 Sept	Llanelli Scarlets	23–6	
18 Sept	Cardiff Blues	39–3	
25 Sept	Ulster	37–24	1
2 Oct	Glasgow Warriors	40–17	
8 Oct	Border Reivers	23–15	
15 Oct	Leinster	11–3	
23 Oct	Castres Olympique	17–38	

31 Oct	Munster	18–20	.
5 Dec	Harlequins	24–7	
11 Dec	Harlequins	46–19	1
18 Dec	Munster	9–13	
26 Dec	Llanelli Scarlets	28–7	2

2005

DATE	OPPONENTS	SCORE	TRIES
1 Jan	Cardiff Blues	15–9	
8 Jan	Munster	10–20	1
15 Jan	Castres Olympique	20–11	
21 Jan	Ulster	22–21	
26 Mar	Edinburgh	29–12	
10 Apr	Connacht	22–13	1
30 Apr	Ulster	23–16	
7 May	Llanelli Scarlets	15–23	
14 Oct	Connacht	18–17	
23 Oct	Stade Français	13–8	
30 Oct	ASM Clermont Auvergne	14–34	1
11 Dec	Leicester Tigers	12–30	
22 Dec	Cardiff Blues	9–28	

2006

DATE	OPPONENTS	SCORE	TRIES
1 Jan	Newport Gwent Dragons	14–24	
3 Mar	Cardiff Blues	14–40	
26 Mar	Edinburgh	24–17	
31 Mar	Llanelli Scarlets	17–30	

8 Apr	Glasgow Warriors	16–13	
5 May	Munster	27–10	2
12 May	Connacht	44–16	
26 May	Ulster	17–19	
2 Sept	Edinburgh	17–11	
8 Sept	Connacht	10–15	
13 Sept	Cardiff Blues	18–16	1
29 Sept	Gloucester Rugby	49–19	1
13 Oct	Glasgow Warriors	31–24	1
20 Oct	Sale Sharks	17–16	2
9 Dec	Cammi Calvisano	50–27	2
15 Dec	Cammi Calvisano	26–9	
23 Dec	Cardiff Blues	24–30	
26 Dec	Llanelli Scarlets	50–24	

2007

DATE	OPPONENTS	SCORE	TRIES
14 Jan	Stade Français	22–22	
20 Jan	Sale Sharks	18–7	
17 Feb	Connacht	31–10	1
24 Mar	Cardiff Blues	27–10	
7 Apr	Munster	20–12	
15 Apr	Leicester Tigers	35–41	2
24 Apr	Llanelli Scarlets	19–6	
27 Apr	Leinster	19–17	
4 May	Glasgow Warriors	26–29	2
8 May	Newport Gwent Dragons	27–13	2
12 May	Border Reivers	24–16	

14 Oct	Munster	16–3	1
27 Oct	Worcester Warriors	47–16	2
4 Nov	London Irish	51–16	3
10 Nov	Bourgoin	22–15	
2 Dec	Harlequins	19–8	
7 Dec	Ulster	48–17	
14 Dec	Ulster	16–8	
31 Dec	Cardiff Blues	22–3	

2008

DATE	OPPONENTS	SCORE	TRIES
12 Jan	Gloucester Rugby	32–15	1
20 Jan	Bourgoin	28–21	1
22 Mar	Saracens	30–3	2
28 Mar	Ulster	32–7	2
6 Apr	Saracens	10–19	
12 Apr	Leicester Tigers	23–6	
19 Apr	Munster	8–9	
25 Apr	Newport Gwent Dragons	16–3	

WALES (UP TO 14 JUNE 2008)

2000

DATE	OPPONENTS	VENUE	SCORE	TRIES
2 Feb	France	Home	3–36	
19 Feb	Italy	Home	47–16	1
4 Mar	England	Away	12–46	
18 Mar	Scotland	Home	26–18	2
1 Apr	Ireland	Away	23–19	
11 Nov	Samoa	Home	50–6	2
26 Nov	South Africa	Home	13–23	

2001

DATE	OPPONENTS	VENUE	SCORE	TRIES
10 Jun	Japan	Away	64–10	4
17 Jun	Japan	Away	53–30	1
13 Oct	Ireland	Home	6–36	

2003

DATE	OPPONENTS	VENUE	SCORE	TRIES
27 Aug	Romania	Home	54–8	2
2 Nov	New Zealand	World Cup	37–53	1
9 Nov	England	World Cup	17–28	

2004

DATE	OPPONENTS	VENUE	SCORE	TRIES
14 Feb	Scotland	Home	23–10	
22 Feb	Ireland	Away	15–36	

7 Mar	France	Home	22–29	
20 Mar	England	Away	21–31	
27 Mar	Italy	Home	44–10	2
12 Jun	Argentina	Away	44–50	
19 Jun	Argentina	Away	35–20	3
6 Nov	South Africa	Home	36–38	
20 Nov	New Zealand	Home	23–24	
26 Nov	Japan	Home	98–0	2

2005

DATE	OPPONENTS	VENUE	SCORE	TRIES
5 Feb	England	Home	11–9	1
12 Feb	Italy	Away	38–8	1
26 Feb	France	Away	24–18	
13 Mar	Scotland	Away	46–22	1
19 Mar	Ireland	Home	32–10	
5 Nov	New Zealand	Home	3–41	
11 Nov	Fiji	Home	11–10	
19 Nov	South Africa	Home	16–33	
26 Nov	Australia	Home	24–22	1

2006

DATE	OPPONENTS	VENUE	SCORE	TRIES
4 Feb	England	Away	13–47	
12 Feb	Scotland	Home	26–18	
11 Mar	Italy	Home	18–18	
18 Mar	France	Home	16–21	
11 Jun	Argentina	Away	25–27	

17 Jun	Argentina	Away	27–45	1
4 Nov	Australia	Home	29–29	1
11 Nov	Pacific Islands	Home	38–20	
17 Nov	Canada	Home	61–26	1
25 Nov	New Zealand	Home	10–45	

2007

DATE	OPPONENTS	VENUE	SCORE	TRIES
24 Feb	France	Away	21–32	
10 Mar	Italy	Away	20–23	1
17 Mar	England	Home	27–18	
26 Aug	France	Home	7–34	
9 Sept	Canada	World Cup	42–17	2
15 Sept	Australia	World Cup	20–32	1
20 Sept	Japan	World Cup	72–18	2
29 Sept	Fiji	World Cup	34–38	1

2008

DATE	OPPONENTS	VENUE	SCORE	TRIES
2 Feb	England	Away	26–19	
9 Feb	Scotland	Home	30–15	2
23 Feb	Italy	Home	47–8	2
8 Mar	Ireland	Away	16–12	1
15 Mar	France	Home	29–12	1
7 Jun	South Africa	Away	17–43	1
14 Jun	South Africa	Away	21–37	1